Sheffield's Time Trail

True Tales from the Norfolk Heritage Trail

❦

Peter Machan

Green Estate Ltd

Published by Green Estate Ltd

Manor Lodge

115 Manor Lane

Sheffield

S2 1UH

ISBN 0-901100-52-8

First published 2004

© Green Estate Ltd 2004

The moral right of the author has been asserted

Text by Peter Machan

Modern-day photography by Steven Brownlow

Designed by Tony Williams and John Williams www.fine-words.com

Printed in Great Britain by J W Northend Ltd, Sheffield

Contents

FOREWORD

I am delighted to see the creation of the Norfolk Heritage Trail and this associated book, which brings to life the rich heritage of the area of the city located between the hilltop Manor Lodge and the Cathedral in the city centre. My family has had a long history with the city of Sheffield since the lands of the Earls of Shrewsbury passed to the Dukes of Norfolk in 1617. When my family first came to the area much of Sheffield was still a deer park with Manor Lodge at the centre. Over the centuries Sheffield has seen many historic events and been involved in many industrial developments of national importance and I'm proud to say that the Dukes of Norfolk and the Earls of Shrewsbury before them have been associated with many of these events.

This book spans the time period from 1571 right up to the present day. The book tells many of the amazing stories relating to these events and developments from the perspective of people who were there at the time, and in doing so also tells the story of Sheffield, including many significant aspects of Sheffield's history that have never been told before.

I am pleased to be in a position to support the Norfolk Heritage Trail and this book as my family have supported the people of Sheffield over the centuries. The 16th Duke of Norfolk donated the Cholera Monument Grounds to the people of Sheffield in 1930, and I am in the fortunate position of being able to carry on my family's tradition of supporting Sheffield by donating a piece of land adjoining the Cholera Monument Grounds that passes through Clay Woods and completes the Norfolk Heritage Trail.

Edward Norfolk

The Duke of Norfolk

INTRODUCTION

Norfolk Heritage Trail

THE NORFOLK HERITAGE TRAIL stretches from the hillside vantage point of Manor Lodge, once at the heart of Sheffield's great deer park and the prison of Mary Queen of Scots, down through the remnants of the estates of the Dukes of Norfolk to the Cathedral in the city centre. Historic sites along the trail include Norfolk Heritage Park, the restored Cholera Monument Grounds and Park Hill flats.

Sheffield is an extraordinary city, with fascinating stories to tell, but the history of Park Hill is the most remarkable of all. There can be few other cities in which you can stand at their very heart, amidst the city centre bustle, and gaze towards a wooded hillside stretching away to a dramatic skyline a couple of miles away. Park Hill, rising steeply to the east of the city centre, from the confluence of Sheffield's two major rivers, the Sheaf and the Don, is one of the city's famous seven hills, crowned by a ridge known appropriately as Skye Edge. With its partner to the north, Shirecliffe Hill, Park Hill creates the dramatic narrow eastern gateway to the city through which the river, roads and railway lines are funnelled and which for generations effectively isolated it from the rest of the country.

Today any mention of Park Hill evokes immediate thoughts of the controversial housing developments that have dominated its lower slopes since the late 1950s. But, of all Sheffield's seven hills, this was the last to be fully built upon, for this has always been the demesne of the Lord of the Manor, and indeed remains so in part today. This heritage is reflected in the names of Park Hill's roads: Duke Street, Talbot Road, Shrewsbury Road, Manor Lane, and Norfolk Road; and the landscape uniquely reflects the fortunes and vicissitudes of Earls and Dukes throughout the ages. Extraordinarily enough this legacy has been held by only four families since the Norman Conquest.

This book is an attempt to tell the story of this remarkable place and its key sites through the eyes of those who lived there throughout the centuries. It follows an unusual pattern, each chapter consisting of a newly-written fictionalised story covering an aspect of the events in each century of the last five hundred years, followed by an historical portrait of the era. The book includes a guide to the Norfolk Heritage Trail and aims to fill out the history of the sites on the trail in their chronological context. It has been commissioned by *Green Estate Limited* and *Sheffield Wildlife Trust*, bodies which have a commitment to preserving, developing and interpreting the heritage of this extraordinary area. The text for this book has been produced by a local writer, Peter Machan, working with school children, Friends' and residents' groups and members of the community. All the characters depicted in this book are real and all the stories, though fictionalised, are actually true, depending on whether you believe in ghosts!

At the back of the book is a map and guide to the Norfolk Heritage Trail, and opening times and location information for the places featured. Look on the map to find the locations for the events described in the stories.

The production of the book has been sponsored by Manor and Castle Development Trust, the Area Panel for Manor, Castle and Woodthorpe and Manor Health Walks. All proceeds from the sale will be used to fund the regeneration of the various sites that they are involved in improving.

$\mathscr{F}$RIGHT $\mathscr{N}$IGHT

October 31st 2003

ALTHOUGH THE COLD AUTUMN WIND sent the brightly coloured leaves spinning, the two young couples hurrying down Granville Road, the girls arm in arm, had no intention of letting the weather put a dampener on their evening out. As always, a shiver ran down Tracey's back as they passed the gothic stone gateway to Norfolk Park and she was relieved that she did not have to pass it alone. Ever since she was a little girl she had found it a forbidding spot but tonight it was even spookier than usual. The silhouetted branches of the great avenue of Turkey oaks behind the elaborate stonework danced in the wind. Above the gateway the sandstone relief of the dog on a helmet, weathered to a skeleton, was cast into sinister relief by the restored gaslight.

Tonight, however, the city centre would be lively with fairground rides and stalls, and Radio Hallam were putting on a roadshow in the Peace Gardens. The lights would be bright, the crowds would be out and Tracy and Mo intended to have a ball.

Intent on their own chatter the four young people did not notice the shadowy figure skulking behind the gothic stone gateway in the blackness of Norfolk Park. But he was watching them, intently. He waited for them to pass, slipped silently through the gate and followed them down the hill, keeping to the shadows and maintaining enough distance to avoid suspicious looks.

'Keep your head down,' Jack reminded himself. 'Don't look directly at them.'

It took all his self-will to avert his gaze but he knew that, on this cold, damp October evening, as long as he kept the hood of his cloak pulled well down over his eyes, he would be safe.

'Aaaghh…' A high pitched, wailing scream suddenly shredded the calm. Jack, thinking he'd been spotted already, only just restrained himself from leaping over the privet hedge surrounding the little front garden he was passing. But the cry turned to a hoarse laugh. 'Gi'o'er will yer nah,' joked the girl, pushing away her boyfriend who was tormenting her with a plastic spider. 'Thy knows I don't like it. I'm not going into town wi' you if yer don't stop it.'

'I'm only having a laugh Tracy. God, it's not going to be much fun wi' you at t' Halloween Fright Night if thy's going to be like this. Thy wants to get in t' right mood,' and he started making wailing noises and waving his arms in front of her.

'Take no notice Trace,' said her friend, 'They're just immature!'

As he hurried down Granville Road after them Jack sniggered to himself. 'Oh no,' he thought, 'there's nothing immature about giving people a good scare. Even now, after all these years I never get tired of it, and I'm in for some fun tonight.'

On any other night of the year the sight of a fully-grown man in a black hooded cloak making his silent way through the streets would have seemed strange to say the least. But tonight he was able to mingle with the good humoured groups of young people, Draculas, skeletons and assorted face-painted ghouls heading towards Sheffield city centre. So long as he kept his head covered and his feet firmly on the ground he should be safe. The pretty girls, clattering along the shining pavement in improbably high-heeled shoes a few paces in front of him, chattered incessantly, while the lads swigged from beer cans. They broke into a giggling run as a brightly lit bus approached and drew to a stop where a number of people stood waiting. Some children wore grotesque masks and a couple actually wore shiny black plastic cloaks. Jack slipped back into the shadows, watching as the queue of people, laughing and joking, made their way onto the bus, the door hissed shut and the bus sped away.

Jack's sharp, foxy-featured face was all alert, his little pointed whiskers twitching and his red eyes glowing. 'I mustn't forget what gets them really scared,' he reminded himself, 'it's when they see my eyes… and, of course, when I leap!'

Jack took a deep breath. It was good to breathe the fresh, cool night air again, after so long hidden deep in the tunnels which, known to the surface dwellers only in dimly remembered folktales, crisscrossed these parts of the ancient manor of Sheffield—from the Castle to the Old Queen's Head, under the Sheaf across the Lord's deer park to the Manor Lodge and even under the High Street of the modern city itself to the ancient Parish Church. It was this subterranean world that Jack had inhabited for eons.

He did not know how long because time had no meaning for him. There in the dark an hour could have lapsed or it could have been a century. All he knew was that each time he ventured into the surface world it had changed beyond anything he recognised or dimly remembered. This time he hadn't even been sure whether he dared venture onto the streets. Even after dark they were lit like day, harsh yellow beams glaring down, quite unlike the pools of light from the gaslights he remembered which provided comforting dark shadowy patches in which he could become invisible. And what had happened to the horses? The streets were familiar but now they roared with the incessant din from the traffic; these sleek metal machines bearing down so fast, with their bright lights like piercing eyes. This was the most noisy, hostile world that Jack had ever experienced, and he would have leapt away and returned to his lair had he not spotted the Halloween revellers and quickly realised that here was an opportunity that had never presented itself before, to slip into the crowd of people unremarked… as long as nobody saw his eyes, his wicked eyes that glowed with mischief like embers.

That was what really terrified the people that had been unfortunate enough to meet him in the past, and there was no way that even the most cunning fancy dress make-up could produce such a startling effect. 'Trick or treat?' He would give them a trick tonight alright, one that they wouldn't forget in a hurry.

Engrossed in these thoughts Jack, feeling more confident, slipped out from the darkness as a family hurried by. Two children were arguing over who was to carry the glowing orange pumpkin lantern, with its gruesome toothy face.

'Cut it out you two or I'm not taking you on any rides at all. We will all be going home again if you can't behave!' yelled their exasperated father but the girl, Charlotte, squealed as Ryan, her brother, poked her viciously with his red plastic trident.

Jack was thoroughly enjoying watching this situation escalate when he suddenly realised that he was standing between two shiny metal rails and that two bright lights were bearing down on him. The mother, swinging round, suddenly seemed to become aware of his presence and let out a shout.

'Hey! Watch out for the tram!' she screamed. At the same instant the Supertram emitted a frightful hooting wail. Jack acted instinctively. He bent his legs, pushed hard off the ground and leapt into the air, landing noiselessly at least ten feet away. His hood fell away and his glaring red eyes shot a glance towards the street.

The mother's blood ran cold and her mouth seemed to dry. She stood transfixed. 'Come on, Margaret. What's wrong? You look as if you have seen a ghost,' said the father, laughing, his arm round a little sheet-covered apparition.

'I can't believe it. Did you see that?' replied the mother, her breath now returning in quick gasps.

'No, I was trying to sort these two little devils out,' replied her husband, 'What was it?'

'You won't believe this, but I think I've just seen Spring-Heeled Jack, the Park Ghost!'

Jack was furious. 'No more fun for me tonight,' he fumed and he bounded in great leaps away, between the dark college buildings, into the brooding darkness of Clay Wood, back to the safety of the tunnels. Safe and deep in his fastness beneath the tall monument that crowns the hillside Jack mused on his misfortune. His world had changed beyond his recognition until he felt he had no place in it. The Park which he knew so well was gone and the exciting times, the time of his life, when the ladies ventured out from their elegant stone-built houses on Norfolk Road in crinoline skirts with men in tall hats, to promenade in starched formality, was obviously gone forever.

From any vantage point up on Park Hill the view is sensational. The city lies sprawled in a great amphitheatre, the rim of which is high Pennine moorland, clearly visible to the west in the far distance. It is a grand vista, and it is not surprising that it has inspired a plethora of both poets and painters. The city-centre buildings below stand in a compact group on their own little hill, known since early times as the Hallam Ridge, rising gently to Crookesmoor and beyond. It was on the lower slopes of this spur, overlooking the Don and Sheaf, that the earliest settlement was established and here that the castle and the ancient parish church were built. From the windy ridge of Skye Edge the prospect to the north extends far up the Don Valley and the view eastwards opens up towards the lower Don Valley and Rotherham.

Gerard de Furnival

Known for centuries as simply 'The Park', this hill to the east of Sheffield was granted by William the Conqueror to the first of its Norman Lords, William de Lovetot, as part of the Manor of Hallamshire. It was he who effectively founded the modern town for, by 1200, the family had built the first church on the site of the present Cathedral, founded a defensive motte and bailey castle where the Sheaf meets the Don and between these two encouraged the little town to grow. The De Furnivals, Lords of Hallamshire during the thirteenth and fourteenth centuries, extended this manorial patronage by rebuilding the castle in stone in about 1280 and later granting a Charter to the little town in 1297. Superb portraits in glass of these, and the other Lords of the Manor, can be seen in what is known as the 'worthies window' in the Cathedral. They were crafted by the artist Christopher Webb in the years immediately before the Second World War.

Of all the great medieval deer parks in England this must have been one of the finest. It had almost certainly already long been in existence by 1281 when Thomas de Furnival claimed ancient hunting rights over it. Stretching over the whole of Park Hill it covered some 2,460 acres with a boundary extending to Gleadless, Handsworth and Darnall to the east, along the Don to the north and from Heeley along the Sheaf valley to the south and west. Most significantly, however, the boundary extended beyond the Sheaf to the west to include the hillside now covered by much of

the city centre, up to the line of the present Norfolk Street. This meant that the low-lying marshy area of the Sheaf Valley, beaded with mills and ponds, was well within the periphery of the Park and provided a rich harvest of waterfowl for the Lord's table. Here the Talbot Lords built their own richly decorated banqueting house beside the Ponds in the very early 1500s. Incredibly, the 'Hawle in the Pondes', as it is called to in the earliest references, still survives as Sheffield's oldest building, now a public house called 'The Old Queen's Head' and incongruously surrounded by the bus station. It is a venerable timber-framed building, but its most surprising feature is the series of five beautifully carved heads which adorn it.

Sheffield then, though generally regarded as a smoky development of the nineteenth century, in fact has a rich history reaching back into mediaeval times.

ABOVE: *The Old Queen's Head, the oldest domestic building in Sheffield and once the Lord's banqueting house*

RIGHT: *Three of the medieval carvings from the Old Queen's Head*

OPPOSITE: *Sheffield Cathedral*

THE ROYAL CAPTIVE

1571–87

G EORGE TALBOT, the sixth Earl of Shrewsbury, Lord of the Manor of Sheffield and Lord Lieutenant of the North, is seated at his writing table in his chamber at Sheffield Castle. He is a tall, thin man, apparently weighed down by the heavy, fur-lined cloak around his shoulders, with care-worn features that would not be out of place on the face of a man at least ten more than his forty years. As he intently scrutinises the documents in front of him, methodically placing them in neat piles and scribbling an occasional note, he strokes his long forked beard. There is a knock at the door and his secretary brings in a newly delivered letter. Breaking the seal and opening it he quickly reads the contents, promptly rises and leaves the chamber to find his wife, Elizabeth.

'My dear,' said Shrewsbury, greeting his wife as she sat engaged in a piece of intricate needlework, 'it seems that our poor friend Henry Babington of Dethick has finally passed away. Mary his wife has written to request that we take their ten-year-old son, Anthony, into our household as my ward since they are our neighbours at Wingfield and here at Norton. I feel duty bound to accede to her request; although this is a difficult time to be taking new members into our household,' he added quickly, sensing his wife's imminent disapproval.

'Indeed it is,' retorted Bess curtly. 'You must do nothing until you have written to Lord Burghley to ask his opinion. The Queen would be most displeased if she found that you had not consulted her in this matter.'

'Of course my dear, you are right. I will write to Burghley at once.'

The Shrewsburys had to be ever vigilant. Since Mary, Queen of Scots, had been delivered into their safe keeping the Earl had hardly passed a peaceful night. The very security of the realm itself was his burdensome responsibility and he felt it keenly. As he had watched the lumbering wagons bearing the Queen, her servants and all their possessions making their slow progress over the Derbyshire moors from Chatsworth to his stronghold of Sheffield Castle the previous November he had felt relieved that she would be under closer guard. But now he realised despairingly the enormous strength of the forces acting on her behalf, for, during the previous month, an audacious plot had been uncovered by which secret letters from their royal prisoner had been smuggled from Sheffield Castle under their very noses to contacts on the continent of Europe by a Papal spy called Robert Ridolfi. The shocking contents, once the code in which they had been written had been broken, revealed a plan involving Spanish forces and an invasion by the Duke of Alva from the Netherlands. At the same time the Duke of Norfolk was to lead a rebellion of English Catholics, marry Mary Queen of Scots and establish her on the throne of England. Norfolk was now safely imprisoned in the Tower, a charge of high treason hanging over him, but the Scottish Queen lay on the daybed in her chamber, not twenty yards from the Shrewsburys.

It was not long before Shrewsbury heard that his petition to Lord Burghley had been granted and before the end of the year Anthony Babington was riding towards the castle at Sheffield. The day was damp and drear and the boy was in low spirits at leaving home. His mood sank ever lower as the grey bulk of the ancient fortress loomed ever larger as he rode down the Sheaf Valley. Grey clouds hung low over the Park and rain trickled down his neck, plastering down his long dark hair. He was tired after his long ride and found himself thoroughly overwhelmed by the thick forbidding walls of the great stronghold that he now approached. His childhood had been spent happily in the wooded dales and hills of Derbyshire that surrounded his father's delightful manor house in the tiny hamlet of Dethick, some twenty miles away. The house had been little more than a superior farmstead and its cluster of barns and outbuildings confirmed this impression. He wasn't prepared to admit it, even to himself, but already he missed his mother and the company of the children of the farmworkers with whom he had been brought up.

Crossing the drawbridge and passing between the heavily guarded bastion towers he truly felt now that his life was changing for ever. To the young lad the welcome appeared cold indeed for he now passed between the rank of grim-faced guards but, gulping down an anxious knot in his throat and taking a deep breath, he tried to pull himself together to meet whatever challenges may present themselves. Passing into the light of the open courtyard within the walls his quick eyes scanned a scene that gave him little comfort. Uniformed soldiers stood guard at every doorway and entrance and he realised with a start what it would mean to live in the same fortress as the Scottish Queen. He would be as good as a prisoner himself!

Suddenly, as Anthony prepared to slide down from his mount's wet back, a shriek of unrestrained laughter tore across his gloomy thoughts. A young girl, no older than himself, ran giggling from one of the stables to his right pursued by a stable lad. She stopped suddenly in confusion as she caught sight of the new arrival and his attendants, bobbed an inelegant curtsey, blushed heavily, and said, 'Oh, beg yer pardon sir. I didn't know we 'ad visitors.' There was the suggestion of a cheeky smirk on the young girl's face, causing Anthony to colour with embarrassment.

A maid now came hurrying towards the group from the direction of the inner courtyard, wiping her hands on her long white pinafore.

'Eleanor Britton, get to your work girl. My Lady needs attending to. See to it at once.'

Without another word the young girl scampered off, clearly in trouble. The maid was flustered as she turned to Anthony.

'I do beg your pardon sir. We have only just received news of your arrival. Humphrey, take the young sir's horse. Let me show you to your chamber, sir,' she said, leading the way towards a wooden doorway and up a flight of twisting stairs. 'You'll be ready for something to eat and drink I wager. I'll see to it now.'

The woman left him standing in a dark panelled room, quite sparsely furnished but comfortable looking enough. Hearing loud footsteps hurrying up the stairway he turned to the door. To his relief a boy his own age came bursting through. 'Hello, you must be Anthony,' said the boy, flopping down onto a chair, 'I'm Henry Talbot. I'm really pleased that you are going to live here with us. You are going to have Gilbert's bed over here. Gilbert went away to Italy after he got married to Mary,' he added by way of explanation.

'Hello, yes, er... thank you,' said Anthony wearily. 'Gilbert, ...married? What do you mean? I thought that he was only a little older than us.'

'Yes he is,' replied the younger brother, 'but a marriage was arranged for him with Mary Cavendish when my father married her mother three years ago. She is fifteen now so Gilbert has to go travelling with Henry Cavendish, our new brother, until he comes of age. They are studying at the University of Padua. Henry is married to my sister Grace, but she is only eight.'

Anthony Babington sank onto the spare bed. There were many things here that were so different from the ways of his careless childhood. He felt overwhelmed and sank into a sleep, dreaming of himself being dragged off to a foreign land to marry someone he didn't know.

Daylight was streaming through the crack between the window shutters by the time Anthony woke. As he became acutely aware of the pangs of hunger in his stomach the same maid that he had seen the previous day entered the room with a very welcome tray of food and swung back the shutters.

'Ah good morning sir. I trust you slept well? I decided not to disturb you last night. You were fair worn out. I am to take you to meet the mistress this morning. The master is away in London presently,' she added.

This was disappointing news to Anthony as his father had always spoken kindly of Earl George whilst he had been aware that people spoke of his new countess, Elizabeth of Hardwick, as a cold, calculating and ruthless woman. He was a sensitive boy and found himself anticipating his meeting with her somewhat ruefully.

He need not have been concerned, however, for Bess greeted him amiably enough in the great hall of the castle. The Countess sat engaged in sewing on a low dais at the far end of the hall. Beside the door by which Anthony entered there was a heavy stone fireplace above which stood the massive carved armorial bearings of the Talbots, the shield in the centre and the great talbot dog bearers at either side. Other stone talbots, their heads resting on their stone paws, guarded either side of the fireplace, accentuating the heavy pun on the Lord's family name. The walls along each side of the hall were lined with richly coloured tapestries, and on a heavy oak table with feet carved to resemble turtles, the like of which Anthony had never seen before, stood, somewhat indiscreetly thought Anthony, portraits of the Countess's previous husbands as well as a thick book with gold bindings set with glittering rubies.

It was clear from her demeanour, as Babington came up to where she was working, that here was someone who demanded respect, and was used to receiving it. She looked up from her sewing, barely casting the boy a welcoming smile and certainly wasted no time in formal greetings.

'The Earl would have been here to greet you himself,' she began, 'but he will be away for some time. We have discussed your position here in Sheffield, however. You and Henry will be attending lessons with the tutor during the mornings and have duties during the afternoons. As you will be aware the Scottish Queen is being held here in Sheffield Castle. She has her own household but I need someone trustworthy to take messages to her and run such small errands. You seem a keen boy. Do you think you could do that?'

Anthony was stunned. This was a world away from the world that he had left so recently in the recesses of the Derbyshire hills.

'Yes, ma'am. I would be honoured,' he replied.

'Good, good...' said the countess, but her mind was clearly already on other matters and, as the interview appeared to be at an end, Anthony made his way out into the bright morning air of the inner courtyard.

He pondered his new position. Would the Countess, he wondered, have been so eager to have him wait upon Mary Stuart had she realised that Catholic neighbours of his father, Francis and George Rolleston, had been so recently involved in plotting to release the Queen whilst she had been held at Chatsworth? It had been a tense time and he recalled his father's anxiety lest the family had been implicated in the plot. Anthony was an astute boy and understood far more of the half-heard adult conversations than his elders realised. Maybe Bess was aware of this and was trying to trap him whilst the Earl was away. Anthony, at any rate, would have to be on his guard.

He had little time to contemplate his new position, however, for when he emerged from the hall into the courtyard Henry was waiting for him.

'Come on,' he began 'Our tutor, Doctor Robinson, says that we can have some time this morning to show you around the castle. Let's start up on the tower,' he continued, running up a flight of spiral stone steps leading straight from the courtyard. The boys climbed three storeys before emerging on the square battlemented roof of the tower that stood at the north-west corner of the castle. Anthony could immediately see why Henry had brought him up here first for it was the highest point in the complex of buildings and commanded an extensive view. Anthony pulled himself far enough over the wide stonework to look straight down at the moat and the river Don passing far below. People passed backwards and forwards over the stone bridge, at the end of which stood an ancient, simple little chapel. Beyond this stretched the hills and meadows of the Don Valley, overlooked by the site of that even earlier fortress on Wincobank Hill. Along the top of the twenty-foot high walls ran a wide walkway. Anthony was anxious to become familiar with the scene outside the great heavy walls so that, in his mind, they did not close him in. The boys descended the tower and followed the curving battlements, which here faced to the south-west and overlooked the little town of Sheffield. The thatched roofs of houses and cottages straggled away from the castle up the hill towards the huddle of rooftops clustered around the tall spire of the parish church which dominated the whole scene. Far beyond, on the westward horizon, the rounded hilltops of the bleak Derbyshire moorlands were already white with overnight snow and Anthony felt a sharp pang of homesickness.

Mary, Queen of Scots

The familiar sights and sounds of a country market with its animals, stalls and traders shouting their wares were nearer at hand only a couple of hundred yards from the great gates. To the south the rivers Sheaf and Porter flowed towards them through lush water-meadows beaded with wide ponds dotted with mills, their wheels churning. One distinctive building stood out beside the track leading from the castle just before the bridge over the river. 'What is that building, the one between the road and the pond?' asked Anthony.

'That's our hall, the one in the Ponds,' replied Henry. 'We've got lots of houses and buildings all around here. I can't wait to take you to that one and show you the tunnels in the cellar. Now, you see all this hill,' continued Henry, leading the way excitedly over the barbican to the battlements on the east side, 'all that is our park. Look, can you see the deer?'

Now here was something with which Anthony felt thoroughly familiar. Many times he had been hunting with his father around the Derbyshire hills and dales and he recalled the times with fondness as he watched the distant herd of fallow deer contentedly grazing beneath the massive trees. Nearer to hand smoke arose from small fires in the neatly-tended gardens and orchards that supplied much of the fresh produce for the castle, as gardeners and labourers tidied the plots of their fallen leaves.

'And that avenue of walnut trees there,' continued Henry breathlessly, 'leads up to our manor lodge in the park. You can just see the tops of the two turrets of the gatehouse at the top of the hill. There are tunnels there too.'

'What's all this about tunnels?' asked Anthony.

'Come on, I'll show you,' replied Henry, disappearing into a doorway in a corner turret on the opposite side of the castle from that by which they had ascended and down a spiral staircase. Following him down the steep stone steps, passing wooden doorways on several levels, Anthony soon became aware that the stairway continued into the gloom well below the level of the courtyard. He could not race as quickly as Henry down the steps for they were so uneven, ancient, worn and hollowed in the centre, and he needed to take every care not to slip. He emerged into a low, dimly-lit crypt-like chamber with a stone vaulted ceiling. His companion was nowhere to be seen. As his eyes became accustomed to the dark, however, he could pick out the shape of sinister looking faces carved from the bosses in the roof and all round the capitals of the pillars from which the vaulting sprang.

'Whoooo…' hooted Henry, from behind the broad column with chevron mouldings which rose from the centre of the room, trying, quite successfully, to frighten Anthony.

'I knew you were there,' said Anthony, hoping that the tremor in his voice wouldn't give him away. The guttering torch that Henry now took down from its bracket was held up to illuminate a particularly gruesome carving with sharp, cruel features and a sneering expression. 'Wow, look at his ugly face. Who is it supposed to be?' 'Oh, I just call him Jack,' said Henry, once more leading the way, this time down the right-hand one of the two dark tunnels whose dark openings led from the far corners of the place.

The tunnel was well built, floored with stone slabs, and just tall enough to allow the young boys to walk upright. Near the start the sides were of rough masonry but after a little way it was cut from the solid rock. It was surprisingly dry and led downwards, fairly steeply at first and then more gently. Anthony, fond as he was of adventures of all sorts, was apprehensive as the tunnel curved onwards and he dreaded the thought of being left in the dark should his young guide run off with the light once more. But the two boys kept closely together and he realised that, for all his bravado, Henry was keen to stay close to him. The tunnel carried on, stretching into the darkness behind and in front of the boys. Although the tunnel was not entirely straight it kept to the same general direction and they passed neither passages nor doors. 'How much further does this go?' whispered Anthony, in a low voice, as if someone might overhear. 'Not much further, I don't think,' replied Henry uncertainly, 'I've only been right through it with Gilbert once before.'

Both boys were more than relieved to see that the tunnel ahead was becoming less dark and soon they could see a gleam of light heralding the far end. They came out into a rectangular cellar into which a heavy iron grating above their heads admitted welcome shafts of light. Stone steps led up to a wooden trapdoor through which the boys tentatively emerged, after listening intently in case there was anyone above. Anthony took a deep breath and looked around him. They were in a light, comfortable-looking, panelled room with a deep stone fireplace and Talbot shields on the walls. It was a richly decorated timber building with windows that looked straight out onto a wide expanse of water. Anthony immediately recognised it as the 'hall in the ponds' which he had noticed earlier. He looked back at the castle walls through the window opposite and realised that the tunnel through which they had come must have passed underneath the great flooded ditch of the moat. 'Come and look at this,' said Henry, pushing open the door and leading outside.

Mallard drakes in their autumn finery of bottle green splashed down noisily onto the nearby pond.

A tall grey heron stood sentinel in the brown reeds and the sound of a water-wheel all composed a welcome, familiar scene as Anthony followed into the bright daylight, though the regular metallic hammerings issuing from the mill were a little mysterious.

'Look,' said Henry, grinning and pointing to an oak carving of a head above the window, 'That's father, but I like this one best.' From around the building five or six carefully carved heads peered down at the two boys. The one that Henry pointed out as a likeness of his father, with its long face and forked beard, was the most severe-looking of all, and Anthony felt apprehensive of meeting him. He felt foolish when he realised that the smirk on Henry's face indicated that he had been making a joke at his father's expense. All the others were of women, one looking like a queen with a look of serenity about her, although Henry now pointed out one carving which was entirely different. It was hideous. The face of an ugly little man was contorted into a scowl. His short legs appeared to be buckling under the weight of some great burden which he carried across his shoulders. Anthony recognised the face. 'Look, its Jack again,' he exclaimed. 'Who is he?'

'I don't know,' replied Henry, 'but I've heard some of the servants say that he lives in the tunnels!' By now Anthony was familiar enough with the joking nature of his guide to realise that this was just another of his attempts to scare him but it made him feel uncomfortable nonetheless when he realised that the boys would have to retrace their path through the dark tunnels back to the castle as they were not actually allowed beyond its bounds without permission.

'Where have you two boys been?' scolded the maid that Anthony had first met the previous afternoon when they finally emerged into the castle courtyard once more. 'I've been searching for you for more than an hour.' Addressing herself to Anthony she continued 'My Lady wants you to meet the Queen without delay.' The boy immediately coloured up and grew uncomfortably hot at the thought that he had so soon inconvenienced his new hosts and that he had unknowingly been led into mischief when there were such important matters for which he was required. He felt angry with Henry but even more with his own foolishness.

She led the way past the guards back through the empty great hall and through a doorway, almost hidden by a thick hanging, beside which stood yet another guard. A curving staircase led them to a landing off which two doors led. Another guard stood at the left-hand door. The maid spoke to him and then knocked quietly on the door which was the only entrance to Queen Mary's apartments. It was opened by the Queen's groom, Bastian Page, a boy of similar age to himself, who gave an exaggerated bow, swept aside and ushered Anthony inside.

He was quite unprepared for the extraordinary scene which met his eyes and stood, mouth open, in the doorway. Here indeed sat a Queen. And around her, her courtiers. The cluttered room was expensively and lavishly furnished with fine rugs from Turkey, bright tapestries, glittering candelabras and well-turned, stylish French furniture. Two foreign birds, which Anthony could not identify, made soft cooing noises from a wickerwork cage and a little black and white dog sat at the Queen's feet. There was laughter and a cultured lightness of air which seemed so out of place in austere Sheffield and was so unexpected in the lodgings of a prisoner. Mary herself reclined on a sofa while her maid, Mary Seaton, embroidered beside her. Behind her hung her cloth of state, like a canopy, bearing its enigmatic motto, *In My End is My Beginning*. The Queen wore a full satin dress of startling red, the colour of which set off her dark hair and eyes. She turned to the boy languidly, smiling broadly. Anthony was entranced. Never had he imagined that he would find himself in such company.

'Ah, mon petit!' exclaimed the Queen, carelessly. But her tone and look were dangerously captivating to the naïve country lad, expressing in one short exchange all the elements of flirtation and experience that her long company with some of the most powerful men of the age had equipped her. How could she ever have guessed that in his innocently-admiring gaze grew the dreadful seeds of that youthful infatuation that would grow into a fatal obsession, and lead to the ultimate destruction of them both.

Towards Christmas the Earl surprised everyone by announcing that an entertainment would be organised for the twelfth night. He had recently returned to Sheffield and hoped that some diversion would lift his dour spirits, for his attendance at court had been onerous. He had been called upon, as one of the foremost peers in the land, to judge and pass the death sentence on the Duke of Norfolk for his treacherous conspiracy on behalf of the royal prisoner who was lodged within the castle. And in the following year he knew that, however much against his will and whatever protests he made, Queen Elizabeth would demand that he was present to witness the gruesome sentence fulfilled.

But now the castle was alive with preparations for the Christmas celebrations. Cartloads of holly, rich with scarlet berries, had been cut from the holly hags that dotted the Great Park, providing winter feed for the sheep and cattle; mistletoe boughs were cut from the tall old poplars beside the river and baskets of sweet smelling apple-wood logs, specially saved from the summer, were trundled through the great gateway. Game of every sort came into the castle: rabbits and hares from the Earl's warren beside the Manor Lodge, hanging in pairs from the warrener's belt; ducks, geese, hens and swans slung in sacks, and three fine fully grown fallow deer and a couple of hogs were draped across the back of a cart. The great kitchen in the outer court was hot and steamy as the bread and pies baked and the meat roasted on great spits before the fires. Servants ran hither and thither, shouted commands rang out and tempers frayed. Silver, pewter and glass vessels, rarely used, were dusted off and polished until they shone. Boards and trestles were set up all along one side of the great hall, which was festooned with wreaths of winter greenery over the fireplace and around the shields on the walls.

As the gloomy winter afternoon darkened, the guests began to arrive in their carriages. Many, such as Lady Bray and Lord Wharton and Mary, Countess of Northumberland, were relatives of the Talbots who lived locally, whilst from Derbyshire came members of the Cavendish family, relatives of Bess, and the Manners, the family of George's first wife, Gertrude. There were local landowners, including Sir Thomas Cockaine whom Anthony knew well as a neighbour of his father, Steven Bright of Whirlow and Sir Francis Wortley, as well as Sheffield neighbours and townsmen of less exalted rank. All were cordially greeted in the great hall by the Earl and the Countess, who looked splendid in a dark velvet dress with lace trim, which set off her pale features. Around her neck hung an impressive necklace composed of strings of pearls.

The Queen, in her cramped apartments beyond the hall sat sighing and fuming, but it had been made quite clear to her that there was no chance whatsoever that Elizabeth would countenance the idea of her mingling with the merrymakers. To make matters worse her guard had been doubled for the occasion. Shrewsbury would take no chances. She thought back with longing to her days at the French court when she would introduce the latest dances and dazzle the court with her intricate footwork. This night was a torment to her beyond the usual restrictions of her liberty. She ground her teeth in fury and strode around the small room in frustration, muttering oaths in French.

In the great hall the guests were now assembled, the wine flowed freely and the buzz of convivial conversation accompanied fine music from the gallery musicians. The supper table groaned under the weight of the confections and Bess especially admired the centrepiece, a great marchpaine and sugar sculpture of a Talbot dog and a Cavendish stag. Anthony sat quietly observant amidst the company of Henry's cousins, quite overwhelmed by the richness of the food and dress. They teased him when one of the servant girls, the cheeky one he recognised as Eleanor Britton, made eyes at him as she filled his flagon and he blushed in confusion.

There was a lull in the conversation as, from outside the open doors, a sound of music grew steadily louder. It was the sort of rough rural music played on instruments that was so familiar to Anthony from his Christmas revels at home, the steady beat of a tabor, the grating sound of a hurdy-gurdy and the nasal drone of pipes. In came a procession at the head of which the boar's head was piped in on a gleaming platter followed by half a dozen gaudily costumed figures, their faces blacked. A cheer went up.

'The mummers,' exclaimed Anthony. 'Look, it's Saint George!'

In trooped the procession of masked players, Saint George, the Turkish Knight and the King of Egypt, to perform the old ritual which everyone knew so well and without which Christmas would not be complete. Bringing up the rear came the cringing figure of Beelzebub, dressed in a cloaked scarlet outfit, devil's horns and a forked tail.

'I am Saint George, from old England sprung,

My famous name throughout the world hath rung,' declaimed Saint George in the familiar monotone, before despatching his several foes whose bodies began to litter the centre of the hall. All seemed over when a truly blood-curdling screech shook the audience into renewed attentiveness.

'In comes I, Beelzebub, and over my shoulder I carries a club,' growled the actor, waving the knobbly instrument with such vehement menace that the audience gasped. He shot a malevolent glace around the room and there were those who afterwards swore that they saw his sharp eyes gleaming red.

'Wow!' said Anthony as the players filed out into the dark courtyard, 'I've never seen a mummers play done like that. Who was that devil at the end? I seem to remember his face from somewhere.'

'I've no idea,' replied Henry, 'It certainly wasn't how they usually do it. I think one of the professional actors in the company that have come for the masque later must have stood in.'

But deep in the tunnels below the castle Spring-Heeled Jack knew better. What fun he had had tonight!

That winter was bitter. The snow fell in great white drifts settling on the castle walls and roofs, rounding their rough shapes and giving the stark old building a more friendly air. Icicles of great length hung from the battlements, the moat froze solid for a month and the water wheels and hammers were silenced. Worst of all was the fierce wind that blew through every crack and crevice. It was impossible to keep warm despite the fires being constantly lit, sending grey smoke puthering from every chimney. But at least there was coal aplenty from the Earl's own mines! The Queen was ill again and did not venture from her cheerless apartments. The cold seemed to seep into her very bones and she wept with the pain of rheumatism. Anthony saw little of her and, in truth, gave her little thought, for the boys, when freed from their lessons, could not wait to get out and enjoy the snow. They would climb the steps to the battlements and wait for an unsuspecting villager to pass by on the road up from Lady's Bridge before pelting him and his donkey with snowballs. On another occasion they built a great snowman in the courtyard, fetched their bows and used it as target practice. On other days they would go out of the castle, down to the frozen ponds where they could slide on the thick ice. When their fingers and toes became numbed with cold they took shelter in the Old Hall beside the ponds, where a great fire was always kept blazing and a cheerful plume of smoke spiralled from the chimney.

The spring and summer, however, settled into a joyless routine. The boys laboured during the better part of each day under the stern tutorage of Richard Robinson, who was also busy publishing his uncompromising anti-Catholic views in a work entitled 'The Rewarde of Wickednesse'. At the other extreme Anthony was then required to serve Queen Mary, who presented England's powerful Catholic threat. It was all most confusing, though Anthony secretly began to feel that his sympathy lay with the ailing Queen who complained constantly of the injustice served upon her. He began to enjoy and value the precious times that he spent in the company of Mary and her household, especially Mary Seaton who spoiled him with choice sweetmeats. He was a quiet boy who listened more than he spoke and he found himself taken into their trust. There became times when he heard fragments of indiscreet conversations which he preferred not to relay to the ever-vigilant Earl and Countess, for the mood in the country had turned sour against the captive. Indeed, had Elizabeth harkened to the pleas of her council during the spring, Mary would have perished along with Norfolk.

When news reached the castle from the Earl in June, that the sentence of execution had been carried out against Norfolk, the premier Duke of England, Mary was inconsolable and took to her bed for days. All of the thirty or so members of her household were desperately anxious lest Queen Elizabeth change her mind under the pressure from her close counsellors. And, shortly after Shrewsbury returned to Sheffield in August, just as things seemed to be returning to normal, terrible news came from the continent that thousands of innocent French protestant Huguenots had been massacred by rampaging Catholic mobs on St Bartholomew's Day, once more focusing anti-Catholic feeling against the dangerous captive in Sheffield.

It had been planned to move the prisoner and the Earl's whole household to the Manor Lodge in the

Artist's reconstruction of Manor Lodge, by Martin Davenport

Great Park during this summer but this news put a stop to such plans and it would be another twelve long tedious months before Mary could savour sweet air once more. Never in all its three hundred years had the old castle been so intensively occupied as over these last years and the smell which now rose from the drains and the stinking moat bore evidence of the numbers who lived within its ancient walls. The conditions had become almost as intolerable as those at Tutbury, the first and most vile of the Shrewsburys' uncomfortable prisons.

By the following summer the Catholic threat had relaxed sufficiently for Elizabeth to allow Mary, under the strictest vigilance, to be moved to the Manor to allow the apartments and the drains at the castle to be thoroughly cleaned. And so, one morning in late spring the drawbridge was lowered, and a procession of wagons and riders on horseback issued from the castle and followed the road over the Sheaf and up into the Park. It was a glorious day and everyone's spirits rose as the skylarks trilled high above them. Nor were their spirits dampened as they approached the Manor for, unlike the forbidding castle, the Manor Lodge was a modern building, built by the Earl's grandfather, with fashionable octagonal towers of brick and stone flanking an elegant flight of stone steps at the entrance. There was no moat or ditch and no great stone bastions and towers. This was no medieval fortress but a comfortable residence befitting the rank of one of England's foremost peers. At the head of the steps stood George Talbot himself, keen to welcome the royal visitor to the house in which he took such a pride. They paused and turned. The view was magnificent, for at this elevation the Park fell away to the north and the little town could be seen in the valley below. Wooded hillsides stretched into the distance. Mary breathed the fresh air deeply, feeling some respite from the long days of her captivity, even though she was no less a prisoner up here at the Manor. The Earl himself led Mary to the left, through the long gallery to the apartments that she was to occupy, partly to satisfy himself that the arrangements made for her security were in place. Although the rooms were small the Queen was delighted to be out of the castle and gazed with pleasure from her window onto a charming garden and fountain in the courtyard. She regarded with less pleasure, however, the armed guards who were stationed beneath the window, in the rooms on either side of her and in the room immediately above.

'Mon Dieu, what do they think I am?' she railed at Anthony, 'Not even a mouse or a flea could move unnoticed!'

Babington sympathised, thinking the precautions ludicrous, but the Earl was only too well aware that his family's continued well-being, as well as that of England itself, depended on maintaining eternal vigilance over the Scottish Queen.

Surprisingly enough, Mary was not the first prisoner of national significance to be accommodated at the Manor Lodge, for in 1530 the great Cardinal Wolsey, Chancellor of England under Henry VIII, was lodged here for some days with the Earl's grandfather, following his dramatic fall from grace. Indeed, it was whilst the great man was under this roof that he was struck down with the terrible illness from which he would die within a few days. Maybe he contracted dysentery or maybe he was poisoned, it was never clear, but certainly he had been in no fit state to travel when Kingston, the Lieutenant of the Tower of London had him hoisted onto a donkey and carried painfully away. The party had only reached Leicester on their southward journey before Wolsey died.

Mary's stay at the Manor on this occasion was, like Wolsey's, all too brief, and she was back at the castle after a few weeks. When she again visited the Manor, however, in the following April, of 1574, she spent most of the summer there and in 1577 she was permitted to stay there from January to July. During these years the Catholic threat was somewhat lessened and the tight grip on Mary was loosened. To her great delight she was allowed to ride across the Park under escort when she felt well enough and often it was Anthony who she chose as a companion. These occasions, together with those when he was allowed to accompany her party to the Earl's house by the wells at Buxton and to Chatsworth were some of the most exciting and enjoyable of his life. He grew to admire her indomitable spirit which never entirely lost faith that one day a solution to her problems would present itself.

It was during the Queen's visit to the Manor in 1577 that the Countess sprung on her a long-conceived surprise. Work on the new lodge building in the manor grounds had been in progress for the previous two years and when Mary's party arrived in the winter it was clear that much work had been done in the previous year, for the three-storied building was virtually complete. A few days later the workmen took down the scaffolding and, whilst they sat together sewing, Bess asked Mary if she would care to inspect the new building. 'Indeed I would,' replied Mary. There was a sparkle in the eye of the countess that was only apparent when she talked of her building projects or of her aspirations for her granddaughter Arbella. Mary was intrigued. Bess led the way down the steps of the Manor and across the courtyard to the new building. Mary, flanked as ever by two guards, accompanied her with a group of her servants. The Countess could ill conceal her excitement.

The stone building had a charming symmetry, its right-hand doorway and three large windows, one above the other towards the mid-line of the building, being perfectly mirrored on the left-hand side. The roof line was battlemented, though the Shrewsburys had no reason to suspect that it would need to be defended, and indeed, the large chimneys and the round brick turret projecting above the roof suggested that they had a far more domestic purpose in mind. Bess pushed open the heavy oak door on the right and ushered the Queen inside. The door opened onto the base of a stone spiral staircase and, to the left, a well-proportioned room, as yet unfurnished.

'Proceed up the stairs, your majesty,' said Bess, directing Mary up the narrow winding steps, past the door on the first floor to the room on the upper floor. Bess was anxious to see the Queen's face as she entered the room for, unlike the lower rooms, this one had been richly decorated and furnished. A bright Turkey carpet covered the floor and the ceiling was a work of the plasterers' art, with geometric designs of fleur-de-lis, roses and pomegranates, lions' heads and the Talbot dogs. Over the grand stone fire-place was the full Talbot arms. In the centre of the room stood a heavy oak dining table. Bess was not disappointed: the effect on Mary was quite gratifying.

'Why, look,' she said immediately, 'here are our embroideries!' In contrast to the bare plaster walls of the lower rooms, these walls were almost entirely covered by the richly-coloured wall hangings that Bess, Mary and her ladies had spent so many long hours executing. From floor to ceiling on the long wall opposite the fireplace hung the newly-completed piece of which the women were especially pleased on which was beautifully worked the representation of the heroine Penelope, flanked by Perseverance, holding a large bird and Patience, with a dog. On the wall beside the window hung a newly-acquired painting showing Ulysses Returning to Penelope. Coming over to look more closely at the picture, Mary was delighted by the exquisite depiction of the young girl sitting at her embroidery in the window.

'Why Bess, you are so clever. This room is delightful, so light and comfortable. It would be wonderful to come here to work on our needlework.'

'But you have not seen everything yet, your majesty,' said Bess, clearly enjoying herself immensely, 'come and see the view.'

Mary followed the Countess up the few steps which led straight out onto the flat lead roof of the building which was enclosed by a stone parapet. The Queen took a deep breath, smiled broadly and threw out her arms to embrace the fresh airs of early spring. 'Why, this is glorious!' she said. Indeed, The prospect was superb. To the south stood the fir-crowned heights of Norton, the wooded vale of Beauchief and the purple moors of Totley. To the north stood the thick woods of Wharncliffe and Wentworth above the valley of the Don whilst to the east the spires of Handsworth and Laughton stood proud of the rolling hills. Bess was immensely pleased, for building was in her blood.

When he was sixteen years old it was time for Anthony Babington to leave the household of the Earl of Shrewsbury. The Queen was particularly sad at his leaving for she had developed a comfortable liking for the young lad who was such a ready listener. A suitable marriage was arranged for him and Anthony travelled to London to study for the Bar at one of the Inns of Court.

There, as one of the few people who had actually met the infamous prisoner Queen, it was inevitable that Anthony Babington should have become something of a celebrity. He was a romantic, flattered to be so courted by his peers and, also inevitably, not always as circumspect as was wise in such dangerous times. Did Anthony not realise that the spymasters of Queen Elizabeth would also be keeping a watchful eye on someone who had been so close to her sworn enemy? Should he not have foreseen that, when a Catholic priest named Ballard sought him out and began to suggest that he use his influence with Queen Mary to take her into their confidence, such plots were doomed to failure? But Babington could not foresee the dreadful fate that would befall them all. He was drawn deeper and deeper into a doomed conspiracy, the details of which were well known to Sir Francis Walsingham's spy network from the very beginning. Every coded letter which Anthony so carefully had smuggled to the Queen in the hollow corks of wine bottles, detailing the fanciful plot to ride to her aid at the head of a party of ten horsemen and to assassinate Queen Elizabeth, was intercepted, opened, read, copied and re-sealed. All that Walsingham patiently waited for now was the inevitable reply from Mary implicating her once and for all in a conspiracy to overthrow the Queen.

Their patience was rewarded when in June of 1586 they intercepted a letter, curiously addressed to:

Master Anthony Babington, dwelling most in Derbyshire at a house of his own within two miles of Wingfield, as I doubt not that you know for that in this shire he hath many friends and kinsmen. The letter was, of course, from Mary, and acknowledged that she was aware of a conspiracy, although it was not until July 17th that the efforts of the spies were fully rewarded when they opened a letter from Mary expressing her full approval of the scheme. As this final incriminating evidence was passed to Walsingham himself he noticed that some unknown hand had drawn a gallows mark on the outside. In this letter he had all the evidence that he required. The conspirators were rounded up and by mid September stood trial on the indictment of wanting to kill the Queen. They were found guilty and sentenced to death. The savage end of Anthony Babington, the young man whose short life had been blighted by his romantic infatuation with Mary Queen of Scots, is not one on which to dwell. It was an infatuation which had brought them both to their ends. The Queen was arrested, taken to Fotheringay Castle in Northamptonshire where she stood trial for treason. George Shrewsbury, as one of the Earls of England, sat at her trial, and when, on February 8th 1587, she was beheaded in the same hall Shrewsbury was required to witness the execution. He sat, head bowed, weeping.

George Talbot was a broken man. The long-held responsibility had seriously depleted his previously healthy finances and had wrecked his marriage, which had disintegrated amidst dramatic accusations and recriminations. For years the two had lived apart, the Earl refusing to be reconciled to Bess and she intent on the building works back at her ancestral home of Hardwick which would occupy her last twenty years and assure her a prominent place in architectural history.

There was one, however, with whom the old Earl found increasing solace. The cheeky little serving girl, Eleanor Britton, had skilfully manipulated the situation of George's dotage to her own advantage and in the last three years of his life he became more and more dependent on her. He had no one else to turn to. Queen Mary was dead, his wife estranged, his eldest son, Francis, had died and he had argued with all the rest. He removed himself with Eleanor Britton to a small hall that he had built at the edge of the Great Park at Handsworth. There he fell deeper under her influence as he grew ever weaker. Behind the old man's back the cunning servant was removing jewellery, money and valuable household items but he was now beyond caring and in these sad circumstances he died on November 18th 1590.

THE SHREWSBURY LEGACY

In 1410 John Talbot, ennobled by Henry VI to the title of The Earl of Shrewsbury, in recognition of the courageous way in which he fought for the King in the French wars, inherited the Manor through his wife. Seven generations of his family were to hold an enormous and far reaching influence on the development of the town of Sheffield, as well as in the kingdom as a whole, especially under the later Tudors. It was during the reign of Elizabeth I that the national spotlight focused on Park Hill, for here was held, by George 6th Earl and his larger-than-life wife Bess of Hardwick, Mary, Queen of Scots; the most dangerous political prisoner in England's history.

Long before this virtually the whole of Park Hill had been enclosed by a deer wall some eight miles in length and a grand manor house, befitting their rank as Privy Counsellors and Lords Lieutenant of the North, was built by the 4th Earl of Shrewsbury at its summit. Sheltered from the wind to the lee of Skye Edge, the site of this house many well have been occupied by a hunting lodge in the Middle Ages. It

Monument to George, 4th Earl of Shrewsbury in Sheffield Cathedral

was here that he entertained Cardinal Wolsey in 1530.

This Manor Lodge was built of stone, timber and brick, with a long gallery and two fine octagonal towers through which the visitor was led up a flight of stone steps into the Great Hall. The whole site covered some four acres, having an inward and an outward courtyard, gardens with fountains and yards.

The superb monument to the 4th Earl, which dates from 1532, can be seen in the Shrewsbury Chapel in the Cathedral. It consists of a life-size figure in marble of George who lies between his two wives. The monument has recently been restored. It was he who was responsible for extending the Parish Church by building the Shrewsbury Chapel, beneath which is the crypt which became the last resting place for family members and close retainers.

The complex of buildings at the Manor Lodge was further developed by the 6th Earl and the Countess with the building of the three-storied Turret House in 1574. This remarkable building, the only roofed survival on the site, was built during the early years of the confinement of Mary Queen of Scots and tradition has long associated her with it. Certainly the richness of the plaster work on the ceilings and fireplaces in the little stone house suggest a use above the mere mundane.

By far the most dramatic legacy of this extraordinary family is the exquisite monument to George, the 6th Earl, who lies, on the opposite side of the Shrewsbury Chapel to his grandfather, in full dress armour and sword at his side. His helms, which were presented at his funeral, still hang from the hooks above.

ABOVE: *The Turret House, the best-preserved building on the Manor Lodge Site*

LEFT: *Interior of the Turret House*

$\mathscr{F}$UNERAL $\mathscr{F}$AYRE

January 10th 1591

T HE OLD EARL WAS DEAD and his funeral was in danger of becoming an unruly affray. It was approaching the appointed hour of two o'clock in the morning of this freezing night and the extraordinary mile-long procession of elaborately-uniformed shield and banner bearers, courtiers, Lords, retainers, servants and family members wound its way slowly from the castle gates, through the Market Place and up the High Street towards the Parish Church, to the accompaniment of the choristers, musicians and the town waits. There had been discussions regarding the correct etiquette to be followed for such an auspicious occasion. By tradition the cortege should set out from the principal house of the departed, on this occasion the castle, where he had lain in state since his death on November 18th, but there were doubts that the funeral procession could be assembled on horseback within the short distance to the Parish Church. This, however, was the course decided upon.

As the pageant-like proceedings wound nearer the church, however, the wisdom of this course of action was called into question, for the progress was all but halted by the immense press of people who had come to witness the spectacle. There must have been twenty thousand folks milling around the route, jostling to get a view and to make sure they were in a good position for any hand-outs that were going. They stamped their cold feet, rubbed their numb hands and pulled rough shawls around their frozen ears. Lucky ones who got there early were stationed near to the brightly burning braziers that lined the route of the cortege. Some enterprising souls had found fuel to light their own fires in the expansive graveyard that surrounded the church. The sound of dirge-like music grew louder as the mourners proceeded up High Street and some of the vast crowd climbed into the trees that grew around the churchyard in order to get a better view.

An expectant hush fell on the vast crowd as the head of the procession passed through the church gates and moved, in as dignified a way as possible, towards the door. But any hope of calm and dignity was suddenly crushed for a cry went up and a fierce commotion broke out over towards the far edge, beyond the great west door. It would appear that one of the fires, built thoughtlessly close to a large tree, had got quite out of hand. Three young men in the branches were coughing and shouting for help. The fierce heat now threatened to engulf them. But there was little that anyone could now do. The on-lookers watched helplessly as the flames roared out of control. With a terrible shriek, each of the men fell from their precarious perch and by the time that assistance could be rendered to the poor fellows it was already apparent that they were beyond human help. A low rumble spread like a wave through the assembled throng.

Within the church built by his ancestors stood, draped in funereal black like the rest of the interior, the opulent tomb of the recently dead Earl. He had himself commissioned the fantastic monument and had spared no expense on ensuring that succeeding generations would marvel at his grandeur. On the tomb lay the elegantly carved stone effigy of George, bedecked in full ceremonial armour with a stone sword at his side. This flamboyant tomb rose to a height of some sixteen feet, all but dwarfing the more restrained tomb of his grandfather, the 4th Earl who built the chapel, and lay more restfully between his two wives.

Beneath the floor of this chapel lay a vaulted crypt, today long forgotten, designed to be the final resting place of the Lords and their families. Lead-lined coffins within this crypt already held the remains of George's father, Francis, and his grandfather, George as well as another five family members. Steps into this crypt led down from the chapel itself from a trap door in the centre of the floor. Shortly the lead-wrapped body of the sixth Earl would join those of his ancestors below the floor, but it was now solemnly borne aloft into the church through the west door and positioned within the extraordinarily ornate structure prepared for it, in the centre of the nave. This consisted of a platform draped with black satin and adorned with the Earl's arms and achievements. Around this were two low rails between which stood nine stools with cushions covered in fine black cloth, on which sat the chief mourners. Above all this stood a canopy twelve feet square, the top of which was draped in black satin and painted paper escutcheons were set at the corners. Along the black velvet valance was written in letters of gold, *Sic Transit Gloria Mundi.*

Whilst Gilbert and Edward, the two surviving sons of the Earl, were making their slow progress towards the Parish Church, the new Earl's wife, Mary, and their three young daughters, Mary, Elizabeth and Alethea, had awaited them, yawning and shivering in the Shrewsbury family pew at the front of the nave. Little Alethea, the youngest, was wide-eyed. She had never been awake at this time of the night in all her short life and it all seemed quite unreal to her. In later years she would recall the event as her earliest memory. As the baby of the family little 'Allathy', as they came to call her, was made much of, indeed there were not many children who had Queen Elizabeth for a Godmother! She had a delightful nature, quick to learn and easy to amuse. Already, at the tender age of five, it was clear that she was a bright little girl with a love of drawing and music. On Alethea's right hand side, between her and her grandmother

Monument to George Talbot, 6th Earl of Shrewsbury, in Sheffield Cathedral

Bess, sat the young lady from whom she was inseparable, the fifteen year old Lady Arbella Stuart, her long white waxen hands, almost luminous against the black satin of her elaborate dress, folded in the lap. As the child of the hasty marriage of Elizabeth Cavendish and Charles Stuart, the brother of Lord Darnley, Mary Queen of Scots' husband, Arbella was in a precarious position, for she had a very real claim to the throne of England. It was around the head of this young girl that all of Bess's intrigues and dynastic family ambitions were focused. Arbella was similarly dependent on the countess, for her father did not live to see her grow beyond babyhood and her mother had died when she was six.

The Lords, chaplains, esquires, stewards and heralds having now taken their appointed places at last, and the eight gentlemen bearers having seated themselves on the stools around the coffin, the Chester herald opened the funeral service by proclaiming the titles of the dead Earl. Psalms were sung, after which the priest proceeded with the communion service, all of which seemed interminable to the little girls in the dark, cold pew. But soon there was more to arouse their interest, for the procession of those bearing the offerings was beginning. The chief mourners and their gentlemen came forward up the centre aisle, led by the Lancaster herald, to present their offerings on black velvet cushions. The book of Coat of Arms was gently laid to one side having been presented by Lord Talbot and Lord Darcy, the target was presented by a second pair of grave lords, the sword by a third and the Earl's helm and crest by a fourth. All were placed with due solemnity in their appointed places. Then Gilbert and Lord Darcy led the procession a second time, each pair coming forward to present the priest with a purse of gold, followed by the gentlemen and the yeomen.

During the long sermon which followed the little girls closed their eyes and slept soundly, Alethea resting her head against Arbella, and it was only when the choir began to sing as it led the priest in procession to the front of the draped dais that they were roused. The eight gentlemen mourners now stood beside the Earl's coffin and took it onto their shoulders. The choir and priest led them up the aisle before turning to the right towards the Shrewsbury Chapel where, to the assembled onlookers, it appeared that they were descending into the floor, for the coffin was carried down the steps and laid on the vacant shelf prepared for it. The gentlemen re-emerged, the stone flagstone that covered the entrance to the vault was replaced with a heavy thud which echoed round the gloomy church, and the gentlemen ushers and porters ceremonially broke their staves across their knees.

Only now, as the procession of mourners emerged from the church to retrace their steps to the castle did it become clear why the event had attracted folks from far and near. Thousands had spent an uncomfortable night in the hope of receiving the traditional funeral dole. The tales of feasting that had followed his father's funeral exactly thirty years before, when fifty fallow deer and twenty-nine red deer from Sheffield Park had been killed and roasted, were legendary. A grey light was already breaking over the Park by the time the great dinner got under way in the great hall of Sheffield Castle. Eight hundred people were served within the hall that morning, most of them honest local folks who had never been in the hall before. There were three courses with eight dishes to each, consisting of boiled, roast and baked meats of the finest as well as bread and wine in plenty. The venison from the Earl's deer park was especially plentiful. The diners within the hall having at last taken their fill the considerable remainder was taken outside and distributed amongst the crowd still waiting. There was sufficient to provide meat, bread and drink for all and to give to the poor the traditional dole of two pence each.

And so George Talbot, the 6th Earl of Shrewsbury, Lord Talbot, Furnival, Verdon and Strange of Blackmore, knight and companion of the order of the Garter, Lord Lieutenant of the Council of the North and Justice of all the Forests and Chases from the Trent Northwards, Privy Counsellor to Her Majesty Queen Elizabeth I, husband to Elizabeth (Bess) of Hardwick, industrialist and entrepreneur, was laid to rest.

If the Manor of Hallamshire was at the focus of national affairs during the time of George, the 6th Earl it was to be no less so during the Earldom of his son, Gilbert, the lad who had been educated at Padua University at the height of the Italian Renaissance. Whilst, therefore, he inherited his father's irascible temperament, the 7th Earl was a man of high culture, with a great love of the arts as well as a particular fondness for hunting. Such were the complications of his father's will, however,

Portrait by Van Dyck of Thomas Howard,
14th Earl of Arundel and his grandson

Life at the castle and at the three Shrewsbury houses in London was conducted in grand style, so lavish a style in fact that the Earl began to be known throughout the country as the 'Great and Glorious Earl of Shrewsbury', though few used the sobriquet to his face! In truth Gilbert cared little for the good opinion of his neighbours or his tenants, and found reason to argue with most of them, but it was with his close family that

that he did not inherit his father's wealth as a matter of course, and the struggles, rows, arguments and outright hostility which the matter of his disputed inheritance engendered kept the family at each others throats for the rest of their lives. Quick to take offence and of a violent temper he was a match for his wife, Mary, who had inherited a similarly fiery temperament from her mother, Bess. Their marriage had been arranged when Gilbert was only fifteen as part of their parent's marriage settlement.

he quarrelled most bitterly, especially with his stepmother. On one occasion, following a challenge to a duel, his brother Edward even conspired against his life. In league with the Earl's physician, Wood, he attempted to dispatch his brother by sending him a pair of perfumed gloves impregnated with poison. The Earl responded in a suitably robust manner by slicing off the doctor's ears! Gilbert's earldom, with dangerous royal intrigues circling Arbella Stuart as they had done her aunt, was every bit as traumatic and eventful as his father's. The facts that his wife Mary had become an ardent Catholic and that she had been unable to bear a son to carry on the Talbot name were additional sore trials.

It was in 1606 that the fortunes of the houses of Talbot and Howard once more became intertwined with the marriage of Gilbert's youngest daughter, Alethea to the penniless Thomas Howard, Earl of Arundel and Surrey. Gilbert had been adamantly set against the match, preferring an arrangement between Alethea and his distant relation, George Talbot, thereby keeping the title and the inheritance within the family. The wishes of his catholic wife, however, prevailed and thus their daughter came to marry the grandson of the 4th Duke of Norfolk, Thomas Howard, over whose execution her own grandfather had presided! The couple were rarely in Sheffield but spent much of their time amidst the whirl of masques, parties and entertainments in the court of James I. The following year the King himself stood sponsor to their newly born son, who was given his name. As godmother Lady Arbella stood in, in place of the eighty-six-year-old Bess.

In 1608 the redoubtable Countess of Shrewsbury finally died, having seen to completion the building work at Hardwick and Worksop Manor. Arbella, the unfortunate niece of Mary Queen of Scots, fretted and fumed, unable to persuade her uncle the King to grant her permission to marry. Released from the restraining hand of Bess her behaviour became increasingly wayward until she secretly married William Seymour, Earl of Hertford, another distant claimant to the throne. Upon discovery they were both imprisoned but, with the assistance of Gilbert's wife Mary, they escaped. Their almost successful escape to France has all the elements of a first-rate adventure. Arbella was recaptured just off Calais and spent the rest of her sad life in the Tower, where she died, virtually insane, in 1615, one of the most lamentable figures in English history. Mary Talbot, for her trouble, also spent two years confined to the Tower.

On the death of Gilbert in 1616, and the subsequent death of his brother Edward less than a year later, the Shrewsbury estates were split between the three daughters. Alethea inherited the Sheffield portion and so the Lordship of Hallamshire came into the hands of the Howard family, completing an extraordinary line of succession, through female lines, from the De Lovetots.

The Shrewsbury Hospital on Norfolk Road stands today as the sole testimony to Gilbert for it was through a provision in his will that money was set aside for the building of a hospital for the perpetual maintenance of twenty poor persons. It was not until 1673 that the alms houses were actually built, not on the present site but beside the Sheaf Bridge. It was relocated to its present site in 1823 and still provides a delightful refuge for its elderly residents in this delightful backwater.

Sheffield's new Lord and his Lady spent little time

in the region. The Earl rose in distinguished service at court and was created Earl Marshal of England. Increasingly, however, the couple lived abroad, in Italy mainly, where using the Talbot inheritance, they amassed one of the greatest collections of classical and renaissance art. Thomas, who became known as 'the Collector Earl' died in Padua in 1646 and when Alethea died in Amsterdam in 1654 their extraordinary inventory of paintings alone listed works by Durer, Van Dyck, Cranach, Georgione, Holbein, Rubens, Titian and Rembrandt. They possessed five Da Vincis, four Michaelangelos and no less than thirteen works by Raphael! Thomas's grandson, also Thomas, was restored to the title of Duke of Norfolk by Charles II in 1660.

ABOVE LEFT: *Detail of Van Dyck's painting of the earl and his wife, Alethea*

LEFT: *The Shrewsbury Hospital, built in 1673 and moved to the present site in 1823*

The Queen's Pocket Pistol

July 27ᵗʰ—August 11ᵗʰ 1644

_____

ITHIN THE ANCIENT walls of Sheffield Castle, which he now held as a stronghold of the Royalist cause, Major Thomas Beaumont broke open the sealed letter and read the communication from the Earl of Manchester with an air of defiance:

The Earl of Manchester to Major Beaumont,
The 27ᵗʰ July, 1644.

Sr.
Being in these parts by the command of Parliament, to reduce such places as yet refuse obedience to their commands, I have sent you this summons that you deliver to me the castle of Sheffield now in your possession, with the arms, ordinance and munitions therein. In the performance whereof you might expect all civility becoming to a gentleman of your quality. I desire your speedy answer, and rest,

Your servant,
E. Manchester.

The Major placed the paper on the table before which he was seated, and pushed back his heavy oak chair. He rose, turned his back on the envoy of the Earl and paced over to look again from the window at the prospect from this vantage point, high in the old castle walls. He needed time to think. His position was a strong one. The walls were thick and the defences were well prepared. He looked down into the eighteen-feet-deep, water-filled moat surrounding it. 'Let Bright and Crawford try to cross that,' he thought, 'my snipers will cut them down before they cross the ditch. And as for trying to tunnel and undermine the walls they will soon discover that its foundations are built into the very rock itself.'

Nor was he poorly armed. The garrison of two hundred soldiers and cavalry were well provisioned and in a good position to withstand a siege until the tide of war turned again, as it surely must, and the besieging rebels be routed. He could easily keep a watch on the comings and goings around the tents and encampments of the Parliamentary forces across the river commanded by Major General Crawford and Colonel John Bright.

'No, I think it pleases me not to surrender the charge that has been placed on me. I feel in no position submit so easily.' He turned decisively to the waiting messenger. 'And as for you,' he said, addressing the bearer of the letter, 'I am inclined to show my contempt for the impertinence of your commanders

Artist's reconstruction of Sheffield Castle, by Martin Davenport

by holding you hostage for their good conduct.' The appalled envoy was led away by a soldier who had been standing in the doorway and shortly afterwards a tall elegant lady entered the room. It was evident that she was to expect the birth of a child imminently. 'Well, Sir, what news of the rebels' demands?' asked Lady Saville, the recently widowed wife of Sir William Saville, the Governor of Sheffield Castle, urgently.

'My Lady, they demand the immediate surrender of the castle.'

'But you have not acceded to their demands I trust. We must hold Sheffield for the King whilst ever there is hope.'

The Remains of Sheffield Castle, now hidden under modern development

'Indeed we must, my Lady, but I am concerned that this is no place for you in your present condition.'

'Nonsense. I thank you for your concern but my place is here. Now that my husband has been killed there is nowhere I feel so close to him. I wish my baby to be born here.'

'You are an inspiration to the men and to all those who are true and loyal to His Majesty, my Lady,' replied Beaumont, who had been left in charge of the castle by her husband.

The determination of those charged with the defence of Sheffield Castle was indeed admirable. In truth, however, their cause was already lost. During the previous month, at Marston Moor, the fortunes of war had turned decisively and the Parliamentary forces in Yorkshire now carried all before them. But if Major Beaumont harboured doubts as to the successful outcome to his resistance as he surveyed the massive enemy encampment of one thousand two hundred foot soldiers and a regiment of horse, he chose not to voice them to the determined lady.

In the encampment on the lower slopes of Sheffield Park the two commanders were pondering on the best approach to taking the castle.

'The castle is old,' argued John Bright, 'its walls are ancient and crumbling. Saville is dead and Beaumont will not hold out for long if we set up a battery to pound the walls.'

John Bright felt at home back in Sheffield. His family were all Puritan, one of the most respected and influential in the region, and lived at Carbrook Hall, the grand house built by his uncle Stephen. John's other uncle was vicar of the parish of Sheffield. He felt it as a personal affront to the honour of his family that the Royalist force under the Earl of Newcastle had so easily been allowed to take control of Sheffield Castle and the town two years previously. He was impatient to take it back.

'I'm not so sure that we will prevail quite so easily as you imagine,' replied Crawford, 'but you are the local man and presumably speak from experience, so we will proceed as you suggest. However I wish you to return to York to bring from Fairfax the Queen's Pocket Pistol and a whole culverin which may well be required to bring this to a swift end.'

And so, under cover of darkness a few days later, on August 2nd, a demi-culverin, a relatively light canon, was drawn up into position by the besieging force into a position in Sheffield market place, only some sixty yards from the walls of the old castle itself. On having had no response to his command to surrender, and indeed having had his envoy taken captive, Crawford was set on bringing some persuasion to bear. To a great many of the townspeople of Sheffield the occupation of their castle by those loyal to the King had been as much of an insult as it had to John Bright. Accordingly, they had welcomed with great joy the arrival of the Parliamentarians, and on this night crowds of them collected in the market to assist in drawing up the gun and bringing turfs and rocks to build a battery across the street to shelter the gunners. Not wishing to miss the excitement, many of them remained around the market place to witness the onset of the bombardment.

Within the thick walls of the castle the occupants were suddenly shaken to the core by the unexpectedly close explosions and the shattering sound of the bombardment of the outer walls, accompanied by loud cheering by the crowds of onlookers. The forces outside the castle walls had, however, badly misjudged the security of their position and let the euphoria of the moment cloud their judgement for there was a sudden crack and a puff of smoke from the battlements. A well-aimed shot from a sniper poised there with his long barrelled flintlock scattered the group around the heavy gun. There was a cry and Captain Sands, the officer of the party, fell with a musket ball in the chest. Further shots rang out and the master gunner also fell dead. There would be no more excitement for the onlookers this day. The canon had certainly caused some damage to the castle walls but it was slight in comparison to the size of the place. It was becoming clear that Crawford's assessment of the situation might have been the more accurate.

On the following day the Major General decided to give the defenders within the castle an opportunity to make terms. He was not a vindictive man. He simply wished to see an end to this irritating episode. Accordingly he prepared to send out a further envoy on horseback, accompanied by a standard bearer and a trumpeter to announce their intention of parleying with the defenders. No sooner had the group ridden within range of the walls of the castle, however, than a shot rang out and a lead ball narrowly missed the trumpeter. There could be no doubt of their intention, for twice more musket balls flew towards them and the group retreated, lucky to escape. On the battlements a group a soldiers appeared, waving their swords and shouting that they did not intend to bargain but were quite secure in their position.

Crawford was furious and sent a further short-tempered demand to the garrison within the walls.

Major General Crawford to Major Beaumont,
Sheffield, August 4th, 1644.

Sr.

I am sent by the Earl of Manchester to reduce this place you hold, and therefore send you a summons, though my trumpeter was shot at, against the laws of war. You may easily perceive I desire not the effusion of blood, otherwise I should spare myself this labour. If you think good to surrender it, you may expect all fair respects befitting a gentleman and soldiers; otherwise you must expect those extremities which they have that refuse mercy. I desire your answer within one hour, & rest,

Your servant,

L. Crawford.

No answer was forthcoming. The tiresome siege would now have to be played out to its end. Over the following days the ordinance battered against the walls almost constantly and the iron works on the Don was kept busy casting the red hot iron into round canon balls. A party of miners was set to work on tunnelling beneath the walls but, as Beaumont had foreseen, the foundations were too massive for them to get far.

On August 7th word came that Colonel Bright, accompanying the monstrous canon called 'the Queen's Pocket Pistol' was making good progress and on the 9th, to the cheers of accompanying crowds of onlookers, the heavy armaments arrived and were set up on a raised platform from which the walls of the castle were well within range.

Before daybreak on the following day Colonel Bright had the satisfaction of watching as the culverin, the demi-canon and the pocket pistol opened up with a heavy bombardment to open wide the breach in the wall made earlier by the sakars. The massive pounding inflicted on the old battlements had a rapid effect as stone and masonry soon began to crumble into the ditch. It was having a similar effect on the nerves of those within the old walls for there was little they could do to defend themselves against such impressive fire power. Suddenly, with a massive shuddering, one side of the great thick wall fell away into the trench outside creating a perfect breach. The Major General prepared to storm the castle.

Faggots and ladders were made ready. But still he hesitated before entering into an affray which would cause bloodshed and loss of life.

'We will send one more ultimatum,' he said to John Bright.

Within the castle the situation was tense and there was a common feeling that all was lost. Many wished to concede defeat not, they said, for their own benefit but because of the plight of the pregnant Lady who, because of the siege, had been denied the attendance of a midwife. She, however, was quite adamant that the castle was to be held at all costs and while she was so strongly resolved, the garrison felt that they could hardly be seen to turn against the wishes of the widow of the governor. For a time they were undecided and returned no answer to Crawford within his time limit but when he opened up once more with the heavy bombardment it was clear to all that they could not withstand for long. Beaumont ordered that the flag of surrender be hoist and sent a deputation of three men to accept the terms offered by the Parliamentarian forces. And not a moment too soon. On that very night Lady Saville was brought to bed and her child delivered.

Seldom can a siege have ended in such honourable terms as were now signed by Major General Crawford and Major Beaumont. It was arranged that the armaments, provisions and stores be handed over at three o'clock on the following afternoon and that, having done so, the defeated force would be allowed to march honourably through the gateway, with colours and drums, and each with his horse, sword and pistol to their own home or to wherever they please. As the crowds lining their route through the Market Place and up the High Street cheered and jeered their passing Colonel Bright quietly slipped into the ruined shell of the ancient castle to take up the office of Governor.

The Earl of Arundel, meanwhile, had long since fled the country. He was well past his prime and would die abroad in this same year. Two years after these events, On 30th April 1646, when the Parliamentary cause had been secured throughout England, an order was issued that Sheffield Castle should be made untenable and slighted. During the following winter and spring the work of destruction was set to with a will. The old castle became a demolition site and local builders took advantage of the ready source of stone, slate, lead, wood and all manner of building materials that were available. Soon the deep moat was filled and poorer properties spread over the site until, by the beginning of the following century, the ancient stronghold of the Lords of Hallamshire was little more than a fading memory.

Ironically the seeds of the destruction of the great hunting park were sown by the lords themselves, notably by George, 6th Earl of Shrewsbury, whose magnificently opulent tomb graces the Cathedral, for it was he, as one of the wealthiest men in England, who had capital to invest in local manufacturing enterprises in his manor. Not slow to realise the value of the resources on his land, he began exploiting the seams of ironstone in the Park and by the 1580s 1,200 tons of coal per annum were also being extracted, bringing in a healthy profit of £65. Indeed, George Shrewsbury was one of the nation's leading industrialists, with a forge at Attercliffe, extensive woodlands for charcoal, numerous cutlers' wheels and tilts along the rivers and an enormous interest in the lead industry from his Derbyshire holdings. So, whilst Sheffield's trade in knives had been long established, during Elizabethan times, local industry received such a boost that it would gradually overtake its former competitors. George had set in train all the elements which would lead to the town changing from an undistinguished provincial market town, with some water-powered industry along the rivers, to one of the great workshops of the world in this smoky nook of the Pennines.

The legacy which the Howard family inherited then was a rich one, though it was not until 1637 that the Earl got round to commissioning a full survey of the manor. This survey, made by John Harrison, still survives, though unfortunately any accompanying maps do not. Harrison lists the castle, four acres in extent, and well maintained with lodging houses, armouries, barns, stables and granaries, as well as gardens and orchards across the river. The Park itself stretched beyond and at its heart stood the grand Manor Lodge. In the Park grew huge, venerable trees, avenues of oak and walnut, and gracing its pastures grazed a herd of over a thousand fallow and red deer. Near the Manor was a warren stocked with rabbits and there were game birds in profusion. The river teemed with trout, salmon and eels, and the ponds, which braided its length, were regularly stocked.

Within the next hundred years all this would be swept away, for the rivers also provided power for dozens of forges and grinding wheels, and below the surface of the Park valuable seams of minerals outcropped; coal and ironstone as well as sandstones which could be quarried and shaped into grindstones and clays which could be fired into bricks. The fine timber was to be felled, the parkland enclosed into common farmland, the splendid Castle pulled down and the Manor house abandoned and ruinous. The river would become choked and the air foul from the smoke of the town's hundreds of forges and smithies which burned hundreds of thousands of tons of the Lord's coal each year. Even the ancient Parish Church itself was neglected to such an extent that by the end of the eighteenth century the whole nave had to be pulled down and rebuilt. Of the fifteenth century church only the spire and the crossing beneath and the slightly later Shrewsbury chapel survive intact.

The ruins of Manor Lodge are a distinctive and arresting sight in modern Sheffield

RIOTS & WRECKERS

1774–1801

I
N SHEFFIELD MARKETPLACE the mood amongst the knots of rough looking characters, grinders, cutlers and traders, that had gathered as the carter had pulled his coal wagon to a standstill, was turning ugly. It was Monday, 'Saint Monday' as it was known in the town, and few of them intended to work today. Some were pointing with the long stems of their clay pipes, for all attention was directed towards the hillside opposite, to the Duke's Park. To the tradesmen who eked out a living in a town where thousands of tons of coal were burned every year in hundreds of forges and furnaces the price of that coal was a pressing matter indeed, and they listened with wrapt attention to what the carter had to say.

'Aye, and what about me?' the carter declaimed. 'When all them wagonways are finished there'll be no more work for me, you mark my words, and you can't tell me that we don't know who will finish up paying for all this fancy development. It will be the likes of us, ordinary folks, whilst the likes of the Duke pockets a handsome profit. Aye, I can tell you, there's not only me as is going to find things a whole lot tougher round here once the Duke finishes building his wagonway with its fancy trucks running on rails. You will find that the price of coal will suddenly go up, and where will you all be then, you tell me that.'

Much nodding and sucking pipes accompanied the carter's words as he warmed to his growing audience. A tide of radical feeling had been sweeping this and similar industrial towns, and those in authority would be wise to heed it. They would certainly learn to do so ere long.

But now all heads turned towards a new source of interest, for a party of fellow townsmen, clearly in high spirits, turned the corner from the Haymarket to cross the Marketplace. They clamoured round a small, thick-set, bandy-legged man, clapping him on the back and congratulating him as if he were a homecoming hero, which to many of them he was. For this strange, grinning character, who looked for all the world like the carved figure on the Old Queen's Head, was none other than Joseph Mather, the self-styled town rhymester, who had just been released from a spell in a cell in the unpleasant little debtors' gaol, just round the corner in King Street. He had been detained there, not for the first time, following his involvement in a drunken affray at Crookes Races a few weeks previously. The crowd joined in the general congratulations for Mather was a popular figure both for his penny broadsides, which pulled no punches in attacking the pompous and authoritarian, and for his outrageous antics. 'Joseph,' shouted one of the crowd, 'What do you think about a man that plans to build wooden wagon-ways from his own coal pits in the Park but won't let others bring their wagons across his land?'

'Such a man,' declaimed Mather,' as would deny the fair rights of his fellow man, has no right to live. He should be strung up high, that's what I say!' A great cheer went up and hats were waved in the air. You could always rely on Mather to rouse a crowd. 'But as for me,' he continued, 'I'm off to the Angel to whet mi whistle. Is anyone coming?' They didn't need a second asking. The group melted away and disappeared through the archway and into the courtyard of the pub at the head of the Marketplace. The coal merchant scratched his head, pulled on his filthy cap and coaxed his weary horse back into life.

On the other side of the street a man of, to judge by his appearance, quite a different calibre, took this opportunity to slip through the Marketplace and up High Street. He had been standing in the doorway of the ancient timbered house at the end of Change Alley and had observed the proceedings with interest and not a little alarm. It was at this stage that he decided not to cross the Marketplace and return to his office in Hartshead but instead to make his way to Fargate to alert the Duke's agent. He was dressed in a manner that indicated he was a Quaker; tall, dark felt hat, a dark cloak, fastened at the neck, white stockings and shoes with broad buckles. Under his arm he clutched a notebook and his assistant laboured under the weight of a polished wooden box with brass corners bearing some sort of instruments. William Fairbanks, the surveyor, map maker and schoolmaster, had been making his way back from the Park. Had the angry mob become aware of his business there, he surmised, he would have been in a very uncomfortable position, for in the notebook was a plan, completed that morning, entitled 'The new Railroad from the Colliery, described and amended to the Plan of Sheffield to the Same Scale.'

Much of the new wagonway had in fact already been completed. It consisted of a single pair of wooden rails, of beech or oak, stretching for some two miles down the hillside from the coal pits near the old Manor Lodge, Jephcock's Pit, Fox's Pit, Greenhill's Pit, Barnes' Pit and others, becoming a double rail on the steeper section nearer to his coal yard beside the Sheaf. It was of a similar pattern to the ones already completed in the north east, and was consequently referred to as a 'Newcastle Way.' When complete the new mode of conveyance would undoubtedly reduce the heavy cost of hauling the heavy loads along the deeply-rutted tracks and so benefit all in the town. But that was not how the suspicious Sheffield folk saw it.

Vincent Eyre, the Lord's agent, recognised all too well that they were a force to be reckoned with. On more than a few occasions over recent years they had turned their anger against various targets. The peaceable Methodists had felt their wrath when their first two meeting houses had been torn down and a few years later high corn prices had led to the Riot Act being read when a mob attacked the granaries at the Pond Mill. He therefore listened intently as Fairbanks related the story of the scene that he had just witnessed.

'And you say that scoundrel Mather was amongst the trouble makers, Mr Fairbanks?'

'Aye, he was there right enough, in the thick of it as usual, although on this occasion I think that it was he who diverted the crowd's attention from further mischief.'

'As you know, the Duke has been aware for some time that there may be trouble. That is why he published the handbill to point out that he has never intended to charge higher prices and that, on the contrary, the new facility of transport will keep them low.'

'Yes, but there are those in the town who are determined to create trouble, come what may.'

It was towards Christmas in the same year, when the long dark evenings gave opportunity for those with mischief in mind, that the surveyor's prediction was played out in a dramatic fashion. The wooden waggonways had been recently completed and the sight of the full corves being smoothly lowered down the hillside on their wooden tracks, to be drawn back up empty to the pitheads by teams of the gin horses was becoming a familiar one. Beneath the surface, however, resentment continued to simmer amongst the disenfranchised workers who would seize on any opportunity to voice their discontent. The match which lit the fuse was an open letter pinned one Saturday night to the Town Hall door denouncing the scheme as a cruelty and imposition and accusing the perpetrators of being 'wicked and merciless wretches'. It was not difficult to surmise the name of the author! An unruly mob began to collect in the High Street and, fuelled by drink, determined to take matters into their own hands. The light from their torches glinted on the rapidly flowing water of the River Sheaf as they passed over the Sheaf Bridge towards the Duke's coal yard where they began to create havoc. A number of the empty corves had been left at the end of the rails overnight. Many of these were quickly overturned and the mob set about the rails themselves. It was not long before a great section had been ripped up. A fire was begun and, with a great cheer, the rails were heaped on. Next for destruction was the wooden loading

Changing times: as Manor Lodge falls into disrepair, a pitwheel shows where Sheffield's future lies

stage and the watch house. There were a few now who began to come to their senses and suggest that enough destruction had now been carried out and that they should make off quickly before the constables appeared. The ringleaders, however, had no intention of calling it a night.

'Let's show his high and mighty lordship, Henry Howard, just what we think of him and his new-fangled ideas,' shouted a thick-set man in waistcoat and moleskin trousers, and so saying he began to push one of the coal corves out of the yard towards the street. Others joined in so that the mob retraced its steps up into the town, pushing the wooden coal wagon in front like a trophy. Reaching the Market-place the wagon was filled with wooden rails and set alight and now, with cheers and guffaws, the crazed mob set about wheeling the blazing wagon up the High Street towards Fargate and the Lord's House, where Henry Howard, the son of the 9th Duke, and his family had already retired for the night. The family were soon roused by the jeering and shouting of the unruly mob outside and when they looked out to see the crazed crowd around the burning wagon they were scared half to death. Worse was to come, for the mob became bolder and began to throw stones at the house so that the sound of smashing glass was added to the clamour and it was only the rather tardy intervention of the town constables that prevented them further distress. The mob now retraced their steps, pushing the flaming wagon back through the marketplace and down Haymarket towards Lady's Bridge. Down the steeper gradient of Waingate the wagon gathered speed and careered out of control down towards the river, the mob whooping and hollering in pursuit. At the last moment someone poked the wagon with a pole sending it veering off the causeway and down into the river beside the bridge. A great cheer went up and the mob dispersed, well pleased with the night's antics.

Henry Howard, his agent and his surveyor stood pondering the scene of devastation the next morning. 'This is the work of rabble rousers from outside the town,' began said Vincent Eyre. 'The same sort of thing has been happening in West Yorkshire and Lancashire and recently in Nottinghamshire a mob smashed the new stocking frames.'

'I'm sure that you are correct Mr Eyre, but what are we to do about the damage here? Surely if we simply repair it the mob will attack it again.'

'My Lord,' said William Fairbanks, 'if I could make a suggestion? I have recently met a young man who is employed in the pit at Arbourthorne which is leased to Townsend and Furness.'

'I have also come across this fellow,' said the agent, 'I believe that he came from County Durham. He has already transformed the efficiency of the pit by laying what he calls 'railroads' from cast iron sections from the face to the pit bottom. The horses no longer have to drag the loads on heavy sleds.'

'We should speak to this man,' replied the Earl. 'What is his name?'

'I believe that he is called John Curr, My Lord.'

And so John Curr entered the employment of the Duke of Norfolk as the manager of his mines in the Park. Having considered the Duke's problem he proposed that the wooden tracks be replaced with a plateway of cast iron, the plates having a flange to keep the trucks on the rails, as designed by James Outram of Ripley. Initially these were laid on cross wooden sleepers but this arrangement once more proved no match for determined vandalism so the plateway was eventually laid on solid stone blocks. Thus Sheffield Park was the location for one of the world's first 'tramways', so called from the name of their inventor.

It was not long before the advantages to be gained by the introduction of Mr Curr's ingenious devices became evident to all for the price of the coal from the Sheffield Park Colliery began to fall. Other proprietors began to meet the competition by investing in similar developments. Curr, however, kept the Duke's pits ahead of the game. He had soon developed a method of raising two heavy corves up the shaft at a time, counterbalanced with two others descending, filled with water. He found that a double flat rope would draw more than double the weight of coals drawn by a single rope and therefore saved the owner yet more outlay. This invention was so successful that he set up 'The Patent Sheffield Ropery' for their manufacture, and in 1792 he wrote to Vincent Eyre:

Sir, I believe that Fire Engines for drawing coals have been introduced and got fairly underway in the neighbourhood of Coalbrookdale. I am of the opinion that these articles are certain to be of great use in our Collieries to take away the necessity of employing so many horses.

The agent agreed and Curr supervised the building of an iron foundry in the Park to manufacture rails, cylinders and steam engines. Soon the puffing, wheezing engines were to be seen drawing the corves at the Attercliffe Colliery and Sheffield Park. The Duke was pleased as profits from the Park collieries continued to grow. As overseer of the mines in the Park, Curr and his family now lived in some style in a house in the Park, leased from the Duke, called Belle View. It was set in twenty acres and included hothouses, stables and a coach house. Turning his attention to housing the increasing number of miners and their families Curr now designed a row of forty-eight back-to-back cottages which became known as 'Colliers' Row.' They were occupied until 1937!

Such a happy state could not continue indefinitely. There came a time when, in 1801, John Curr was asked to a meeting with Vincent Eyre.

'These are difficult times, Mr Curr. The Duke's mines are no longer making the profit that they were some years ago. The Attercliffe pit, as you know, needs constant pumping as water from the nearby River Don continues to pour down the workings. Older pits in the Park have hit geological difficulties and the depression in trade and the opening of the new pits at Handsworth and Darnall has meant that the market will not stand a rise in prices that would make the workings economic.'

'I am only too well aware of the present difficulties, Mr Eyre. I am having problems meeting the higher cost of hay and corn to say nothing of the enormous increase in the men's wages.'

'Over the years you have performed great service to the Duke,' said Mr Eyre, 'and he is very anxious that you recognise his gratitude.'

'I have always done my best to serve his Lordship,' replied Curr, unsure where this uncomfortable discussion was leading. 'Bad as the collieries have lately proved, they would have been worse if I had not made the improvements which we have carried out.'

'Yes, quite so, but now the Duke feels that it is time to make a change and to see whether another could alter his fortunes.'

'I see,' said the crestfallen Curr.

And so, for reasons which appeared to be entirely beyond his control, John Curr, the man who had built up a national reputation as one of the country's foremost mining engineers, was dismissed from the service of the Duke and the story of his great contribution to industrial development was largely forgotten.

Whilst Hallamshire's lords still retained an enormous influence over the town's affairs this was generally conducted through their agents and the Dukes themselves chose not to live here. Throughout the seventeenth and eighteenth centuries the Howards, restored to their title of the Dukes of Norfolk in 1660, paid little more than fleeting visits to Sheffield, preferring to concentrate their attention in this area on the building of their manor at Worksop. There was, therefore, the opportunity for the cutlers and tradesmen to begin to administer their own affairs. They wasted little time, establishing the Cutlers Company in 1624.

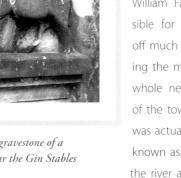

Old Steady: *the gravestone of a favorite horse near the Gin Stables*

Although the lords were still keen to exploit the rich economic potential of their manor of Hallamshire, this being their most valuable asset, the cutlers, steelmakers, silversmiths and platers themselves generated the commercial developments which were to transform the little market town into an industrial powerhouse.

It was not until the time that Henry Howard, the 11th Duke of Norfolk, held the title from 1786 that a leading member of the family began to take a prominent role in the town's development. He and his family had lived in 'The Lord's House' on Fargate since 1764 before moving to Darnall Hall in 1780. It was Henry and his agent, Vincent Eyre, who, with the help of the surveyor, William Fairbanks, were responsible for enclosing and selling off much of their estate, rebuilding the markets and planning a whole new fashionable quarter of the town, only part of which was actually built, the area, then known as Alsop Fields, between the river and Norfolk Street. The gridiron street plan and the names themselves, Howard Street, Eyre Street, Arundel Street, clearly identify this part of the town, and a few of the elegant town houses, preserved through their subsequent use as cutlery factories, still stand on Arundel Street. On the opposite side of the river, in the Park, a truly extraordinary man

ABOVE: *Miners' homes built around the ruins of Manor Lodge*

was developing the lord's mining interests as Superintendent of the park collieries; Sheffield Park Colliery, at the bottom of the hill, Wood Pits Colliery a little further up and Manor Colliery within the very precincts of the Shrewsbury's manor house itself. John Curr was a mining engineer who here pioneered innovations which would make these collieries some of the most technologically advanced in the country.

The Gin Stables on Stafford Road were built by the Duke in the eighteenth century to accommodate the horses which served in the Park pits. They have recently been converted into mews cottages. A remarkable gravestone to one of the horses is built into one of the walls.

LEFT: *The Gin Stables, now private dwellings*

CHOLERA MORBUS

July–October 1832

'COME AWAY, Mercy! Quickly girl!'

'Ow, mama that hurts, you're pulling my arm.'

But being gentle with little Mercy is not Elizabeth Smith's main concern at this moment. She grabs the little girl and pulls her back from the edge of the muddy roadway of South Street. As a wagon lumbers slowly past them up the hill, the horse pulling laboriously against the gradient, the wooden wheels clatter over the rutted surface and part of one of the parcels wound up in dirty sheets which are piled on the back flops over the side, revealing a pale, dead hand. The mother lets out a gasp and clutches the children tightly to her, attempting to cover their faces. But five year old Mercy struggles free from the rough folds of her mother's long skirt and watches, wide eyed and fascinated as the tall thin man who accompanies the load hastily pushes the bundle back, holding a large handkerchief to his face. Following the wagon now comes a mournful procession, families of the unfortunate Cholera victims who were being so hurriedly and unceremoniously transported for burial. Ragged, barefoot children, woollen shawled mothers cradling babies, and fathers, still in their working clothes, anxious not to lose too much time from the grinding wheel.

'What is it, mama?' asks Mercy, as usual alert and inquisitive.

'Oh Mercy, it's the Cholera Basket,' replied her mother. 'The poor souls are being taken to the burial ground up the hill.'

'What's cholera?' asked little Mercy.

'It's a terrible disease Mercy, that's taking poor people as fast as they can bury them.'

'Why is it, mama?'

'Oh Mercy I'm sure I don't know. As if there aren't enough ills and diseases in Sheffield without another one.'

Like most mothers Mrs Smith was only too well acquainted with the terrible consequences of their poverty. The children and their mother now hurriedly made their way back to their courtyard cottage on the other side of South Street. It was only a few months ago that they had lost little George, and Anne, the eldest girl, who at twelve years old was working as a buffer in one of the new cutlery factories, had developed a cough that might indicate consumption.

It was towards evening when Mercy's father and her ten-year-old brother arrived home, their wooden clogs clattering on the cobbled yard. Mercy, who had been playing at funerals, wrapping her peg doll in a scruffy piece of material and placing it in her old soapbox, ran to meet them excitedly. As usual she couldn't wait to tell them the news of the day, and today had been particularly exciting. Her father, however, filthy from the dust thrown up from the grindstone over which he sat hunched all day, greeted her news with a grim face as he splashed the grey water from the pump in the yard over his arms and face.

'Aye, and from what I hear in the town it's getting worse. There were twelve buried today and the doctors can't do a thing about it. The poor souls seem to be fit and well one day and dead the next. I've never seen anything like it.'

He sat down at the scrubbed wooden table as a plate of boiled potatoes and bread was placed in front of him.

'I hoped that it was going to miss Sheffield. They say now that it came from Sunderland and that the first people to catch it came off a ship from the East. They've had a terrible time of it in Liverpool and Leeds and now it looks like we're in for it.'

'Oh William, is there nothing we can do to guard the children against it?' asked his anxious wife.

William Smith spoke with a low, tired voice. 'No lass, I don't think there is. They don't seem to have any idea what causes it, but I can tell you that most of the folks that have been struck down have come from the bottom end of the town. It's folks like us that it seems to take.'

'Oh William, don't talk like that,' replied his despairing wife, 'we will do everything we can to keep the little ones safe.'

'Aye, I'm sure we won't come to any ill,' comforted her husband. But he was none too sure.

It was a warm day in the middle of August and James Montgomery, well known in Sheffield as the editor of *The Iris* had taken an unusual hour's break to stroll up through the Park to call on John Holland at his secluded cottage near the ruins of the old Manor. The two men sat on the wooden seat beneath the pear tree at the front of the cottage on which they had so often discussed the progress of one or other of their poems. Yes, poems! In a town like Sheffield this was indeed an unusually intellectual pair; Montgomery, whose hymns and poems were now so popular throughout the country, and Holland whose private income made it possible for him to write on whatever subject he turned his attention to.

'James, it really won't do. Surely we can't have corpses bundled about the town on the back of a cart, even if this is an emergency! You know what people are calling it, 'The Cholera Basket.' Really sometimes I begin to despair of how things are managed in Sheffield. Can't you write an article about it in your newspaper next week?'

'Don't worry, John, It's already been arranged. I was as concerned as you when I heard about the undignified way in which the dead were being treated, with no regard to the finer feelings of their kin. As the new Chairman of the Board of Health I have now arranged for the bodies to be transported to the new burial ground in a covered conveyance.'

'Look at it James. Is it any wonder that the poor people are ill? Even in the summer heat the pall of smoke hangs over the town like a black veil. The people are sickly before they are even infected with the disease. What chance do they have?'

'I know. I walked up the hill from my office. The conditions that families are being brought up in are sometimes not fit for a dog. As you come over the Sheaf bridge the smell of sewage is appalling, especially in this weather when the river is so low. And yet I see that there is yet more building. The town is growing so quickly that I hardly recognise it from when I came here forty years ago.'

'Yes, and what changes we have seen in that time. I always thought that up here, amongst the fields and woods of my beloved park, I was remote from the affairs of the town but I sometimes think that even here I am not safe from the relentless march of bricks and mortar!'

Holland turned his attention to the woeful news carried in the pages of the weekly newspaper that Montgomery had brought him from the town.

We regret deeply that after 20,000 cases of cholera in this country, began the article, *the disease is nearly as little understood as at its first appearance. The evils of cholera in this neighbourhood have been exceedingly aggravated by intemperance and profligacy in both sexes!*

'Oh really James!'

'I know what you mean. The way that *The Mercury* has been reporting the epidemic is sensational and heartless. It's not surprising that people are panicking about it. Listen to this:

Those who are dying are either persons of intemperance or filthy habits or are brought to the hospital in the last stages of the disease. One girl who died was a great opium eater, although only 11 years old. A few days ago a woman, having returned to her home, slept in a bed in which her brother had died recently. Although the bed had been carefully washed the poor woman was attacked by cholera during the night. In 30 hours she was a corpse.

'Doctor Holland at the cholera hospital is doing a splendid job but when poor children and adults who are already weakened by their poor diet and hard work are brought in there is little he can do to save them. How can he fight the infection if we still don't understand the causes of the disease and when people are spreading such terrible rumours about the doctors?'

'What rumours are these, James?'

'Oh, there are foolish people who are saying that, far from helping the sick to recover, the medical people at the House of Recovery are actually hastening their deaths in order to sell the bodies for medical research. There is also a great fear generally that sufferers are being buried before life is quite extinct. There was almost a riot down here in the Park last Wednesday when the medical attendants who had called to transport a sick patient to the House of Recovery were set upon by a group of persons who swore and insulted them.'

'And I have heard that there are still many people who refuse to believe that the disease has broken out in Sheffield at all!'

'Not to mention those who have taken the outbreak as an excuse for the most debauched and drunken behaviour!' replied Montgomery as he collected his stick and hat and rose from the seat. 'But I must be on my way,' he continued, 'I mean to call on Michael Ellison at The Farm to discuss with him something which I wish to bring up at tomorrow's weekly meeting of the Board of Health at the Cutler's Hall.'

'What's that James?'

'I wish to put forward the idea of holding a day of fasting and supplication for the remission of the dreadful disease,' replied Montgomery.

At The Farm, Michael Ellison, the agent of the Duke of Norfolk, was engaged on writing a reply to his father who, having read of the outbreak of disease in Sheffield, had written to urge him to leave the town with his family. Nor had his father been the only one to give such wise advice. His doctors had been of the same opinion. But how could he? His duty, he felt, was clear. The leaders of the town must set an example. And so, every week since the first case had been confirmed in June, he had met with James Montgomery, John Blake, the master cutler, and Henry Doncaster, one of the town's leading industrialists, and others as the Board of Health, and, sickening and depressing though he found the duty, he intended to see it through.

I hear that you are feeling anxious about us at this awful time, he begins*, but I am happy to tell you that although the pestilence has raged through this town with great fury it has pleased providence that we should have escaped. We have had a few alarms, however, for every symptom of derangement of the digestive organs has been liable to be construed as a premonitory sign of this horrible disease. Both our servants have been unwell and have been obliged to have medical aid, and I have little doubt that, if their cases had been neglected, cholera would have ensued. With the concurrence of the Duke of Norfolk, I allotted a piece of ground as a burial place for those carried off with the pestilence. It was difficult to fix upon a spot for this purpose as no person was willing that it should be near their residence. To silence all objection I was obliged to bring it to my own neighbourhood and set out a piece of land at the top of the hill on the north side of my house, in front of the new Shrewsbury hospital buildings.*

The door opened and Elizabeth, his wife entered. 'My dear, Mr Montgomery has called to see you,' she said, showing the visitor in.

'James, good afternoon. I'm pleased to see you well.'

'Yes, thank the Lord.'

'Indeed,' replied Ellison, 'please take a seat. I have been looking at the numbers of burials during the last week,' he said, turning to pick up a sheaf of papers from the desk, 'I think you will be shocked.'

'The bell of the Parish Church has been tolling constantly so I knew that the situation was bleak.'

'Far worse than any before, James. During the second week of August a hundred and ten victims were buried.'

'One hundred and ten!'

'Yes, indeed. I think the figure will shock everyone at tomorrow's meeting. The disease has been sweeping through whole areas. Thirty-seven of that total came from the lower Park. The courtyards on South Street have been struck particularly heavily.'

'Do you consider that they have been at risk from the miasma exuded from the bodies as they are carried up to the burial ground?'

'Who knows, James. Our new hearse should solve that problem anyhow. But the most recent medical opinion seems to be that the disease is contracted by ingesting some agent in contaminated water.'

'Well, I am a religious and not a medical man,' replied Montgomery, 'but there is no doubt that it is those who live in the greatest filth who are being struck down. We must turn to God and put our faith in him to relieve the sufferings of our fellow townspeople.'

Montgomery proceeded to put to the agent his idea for the day of supplication and at the meeting of the Board on the subsequent day it was decided that August 22nd should be so designated. John Blake, whose happy duty it had been at the start of his term of office earlier in the year, to lay the foundation stone of the new Cutler's Hall, was particularly enthusiastic to take any action whatsoever which might alleviate the suffering in the town.

There was little more that the family of little Mercy Smith, in their poverty-stricken courtyard, could do than pray for their safe deliverance, though they had little cause to have any real faith in their success. The warm weather had made the summer particularly uncomfortable for the smell from the overflowing privies across the court and the pigs in the adjoining yard became almost unbearable. It had also meant that the pump in the yard, drawing water from a shallow well, had dried almost to a trickle of brackish water. In South Street the real terror, however, had not begun until August 11th when James Taylor, an

PROPOSED MONUMENT FOR THE CHOLERA CEMETERY AT SHEFFIELD.

Original lithograph sold to raise funds for the building of the monument

older man, but fit and strong, whose hammer could normally be heard ringing on the anvil in the forge across the yard all day long, was suddenly stricken down. His anvil was ringing one day as usual and the next it rang no more, for James was on his way up the street to the burial ground. On the same day John Brook and nine year old Cicely Arnold were similarly carried off, and on the following days the sound of loud weeping and wailing came from one stricken family or another in the street, whilst their neighbours held their breath and hugged their children ever tighter. August 12th was especially difficult, for Mary Grayson, a mother with five children, died as well as fourteen-year-old Grace Raynor and two girls of twenty one, close friends. On the 13th Henry Dalton was carried off, leaving his family destitute, and on the 14th another three South Street families buried dead members. The next day saw only one death in the road and on the following two days it appeared that the epidemic had run its course. On the morning of the 18th however, little Mercy had a high temperature, by lunchtime she was delirious and vomiting and by tea-time the poor little mite had died.

The fever continued to rage through the packed and insanitary lanes and alleys of the Park; Collier's Row, the Ropery and Duke Street in particular, though after the death of old William Mitchell on the 23rd the residents of South Street were spared any further grief. The whole town was shaken, however, by the shocking news that awaited the members of the Board of Health when they arrived at the Cutlers Hall for their weekly meeting on September 1st, only to find the doors locked and the place in mourning. Michael Ellison met James Montgomery with the terrible news,

'Good morning Mr Ellison,' said Montgomery, doffing his hat to greet the agent. Ellison was white faced and drawn. 'What is it? Has something happened?'

'James, have you not heard yet? Blake is dead!'

'What! I was with him only yesterday morning. Surely he can't have contracted the cholera.'

'I'm afraid that he did, James. He was taken ill shortly before lunch yesterday and the terrible disease took a particularly rapid course. Poor John died after only a few hours' illness.'

'God rest his soul.'

There was no elaborate funeral service at the Parish Church in memory of the stricken Master Cutler. Like all the other victims he was hurried to the common burial ground, along with two children, Jane and Charles Hawksworth, and four others who died on the same day. There were not a few in the town who were forced to reassess their high-principled view that the disease was a visitation from God on the dirty, idle and immoral.

After the first few days of September the weather turned cooler, the people at last began to see the effectiveness of seeking aid at the onset of any symptoms and the death toll rapidly fell. Only four more people fell victim in September and on October 11th the last two bodies were deposited in the burial ground. A little over four hundred Sheffielders had died. Three hundred and thirty-nine lay in the small space of the burial ground opposite the Shrewsbury Hospital on Norfolk Road.

For two years the ground where the victims had been buried lay rough and unkempt. Michael Ellison had been very badly shaken by the experience and wished to put the whole matter behind him. Montgomery, however, was far from satisfied at the thought that most of the dead had no memorial and broached the subject at the final meeting of the Board of Health, almost exactly two years after it had been established,

'As Chairman of the Board of Health, I would like to put it to you, gentlemen,' began Montgomery, 'that the hundred pounds which Mr Ellison, the treasurer, has from the auction of the surplus goods at the hospital be put together with money which, I suggest, could be collected by subscription, to level and fence the burial ground and to erect a fitting memorial to testify the gratitude of the living, by a commemoration of the dead, when they were spared and the latter were taken away.'

'I would second Mr Montgomery's suggestion,' said Michael Ellison. 'I have already spoken of it to the Duke of Norfolk and he expressed his wish to make a liberal contribution towards the cost.'

'And I believe that you have in mind someone who could help us with the design of a suitable monument?'

Ellison opened a large folder on the table in front of him and took out a drawing of a startling structure. 'My young nephew, Matthew Hadfield, is quite a talented architect and he has become extremely interested in this project. I have taken the liberty of bringing along a design of his that I think has some merit.'

The drawing, which Ellison now displayed, was of a tall, slender, triangular gothic shaft, some seventy feet high, surrounded by graceful exotic trees, overlooking the town and the hills beyond. It was a fine concept and the Board were immediately captivated.

'How much does Hadfield think that this would cost?' asked Henry Doncaster.

'He thinks that it can be done for three hundred pounds. He is willing to have this drawing made into an engraving at his own expense and to sell copies around the town to help raise the funds.'

And so it was agreed, the funds were quickly assembled and on December 11th the Board met on the site to lay the foundation stone of the memorial. Following a few prayers led by Montgomery, Michael Ellison laid, into a cavity in the stone, a bottle containing a paper that gave a description of the course of the disease. Work on the monument carried on through the winter and by April of 1835 the graceful shaft, complete with its three figures and topped with a cross, soared above the skyline of Clay Wood. Matthew Hadfield surveyed the completed project with satisfaction. 'I hope sir, your work of this day will be permanent' he remarked to Montgomery.

'May it stand till the day of Resurrection,' replied the poet.

The few houses that were to be found on the lower slopes of Park Hill in the early eighteenth century were still set amongst green fields, a good way beyond the built up area of the town itself. This was a small and close-knit community of cutlers, farmers and miners who seldom ventured further than Sheffield market. They married mostly amongst themselves and they helped one another on the occasion of the death of a breadwinner, an all too familiar event in a town where the expectation of life was short. Under the stimulus of the Napoleonic wars in the early years of the nineteenth century trade prospered and, with the opening of the canal at the foot of the hill in 1822, markets expanded, especially for the Duke's coal. Shoddily-built properties

The Cholera Monument as it is today

were quickly constructed to house the rapidly expanding population that was migrating from the countryside. Some, like Collier's Row, were built specifically to house the miners and were some of the earliest examples of industrial housing. By 1820 the lower slopes of Park Hill became a warren of courtyard and back-to-back cottage properties densely packed on different levels. The houses seemed, from a distance, to have been built on top of one another. The lanes and alleyways were linked by long flights of stone steps or steep hills.

Life in Sheffield was tough generally, but here the living conditions became unspeakable. Around unsavoury courtyards were packed single room whitewashed cottages in which whole families lived out their lives in utter

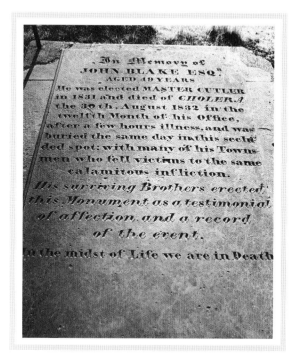

The gravestone of John Blake, Master Cutler

squalor. Disease was rife; typhus, typhoid and malaria were killers, and in 1832 the dreaded Asiatic cholera was brought to the town, killing over four hundred Sheffielders in three months. Their bodies were hastily buried in a communal graveyard on a piece of land in the Park given by the Duke of Norfolk. Only the grave of the serving Master Cutler, John Blake, was afforded the distinction of a gravestone but money was raised by subscription organised by James Montgomery the hymn writer to erect the monument, which has recently been restored, on the site of the burials, overlooking the town. The fine memorial to Montgomery himself now stands beside the Cathedral. Of the 292 burials, which were recorded in the Cholera Burial Ground between August 3rd and October 11th, no less than sixty-two were members of the little community at the foot of Park Hill.

NEVER A PROUDER DAY

May 21st 1897

'Never in all our city's story, rose the sun on a prouder day'

DOWNSTAIRS, THE BELL rang insistently. Up in the servants' quarters at Laithfield House on Norfolk Road, the young girl adjusted her white cap, brushed down her spotlessly white apron and hurried down the back stairs in response to its calling. As she came through the hallway she glanced up at the box that showed which bell had summoned her. The white marker indicated that it was the drawing room bell that had been pressed and she accordingly entered.

'Ah, Emily. There you are,' said the lady of the house, Rebecca Kaye, lowering the copy of the *Sheffield and Rotherham Independent* that she was reading and removing her spectacles. She was elegantly dressed, in a long green taffeta gown with a high collar, which rustled as she moved. Still not yet thirty, she lived in some style, for her husband had a good business as the major fruit and vegetable wholesaler at Sheffield market. Their large semi-detached stone villa, standing in its extensive well-manicured gardens on Norfolk Road, was more typical of those in Broomhill than Park Hill.

'Yes, ma'am?'

'You know that the Queen will be coming to Sheffield to open the Town Hall on the 21st, that's a week on Friday?'

'Oh yes, ma'am. Everyone's talking about it. They say that Queen Victoria is the first Queen to come here since Mary Queen of Scots.'

'Well, yes I suppose she is,' replied Emily's employer with a smile, 'but do you realise that the procession will be coming along this road, right in front of the house?'

'No!' said Emily, wide-eyed, 'Why is that?'

'It seems that we are on the official route,' replied Mrs Kaye, referring to a report in the paper. 'When the Queen has opened the Town Hall she will be going through Norfolk Park, where all the children are going to sing, and then she will be coming down Norfolk Road on the way to the Cyclops Steel works. Isn't that exciting!'

Indeed it certainly was. Emily, having seen all the preparations for the royal visit in town and having heard little else from her young sister for weeks past, had been feeling thoroughly miserable at the thought that she was going to miss all the excitement. But now it looked as if she would be having a ringside seat! She couldn't contain her excitement. 'Oh ma'am, that's wonderful. Fancy, the Queen, coming past our house. Just wait till I tell my sister Alice. She will be going with her school to sing in the park. She's been driving my mother daft singing one of the songs called "Diamond Reign" but she made us laugh because she didn't understand the words and she said 'I hope it doesn't rain for the Queen!'

'Oh yes, Bessie and Geoffrey have been practising that. We've been singing it round the piano in the evenings. Did you know that it had been specially written? It should sound marvellous when every child in the city is there singing their hearts out!' Mrs Kaye laughed. 'But isn't your father involved in the visit as well?'

'Yes ma'am, he is. He's a steel melter at Cammell's. The Queen will be going to see one of the big steel plates being rolled. He's got to help to pull it out of the furnace,' she replied with obvious pride. 'And I'd better get to work. If Queen Victoria is going to come along the road this house is going to do us proud!'

'Alice Burgin. Are you listening?' boomed the stern voice of Miss Stanley, the headmistress of Park Board School where seven-year-old Alice was a pupil. 'How dare you shuffle around like that while I am giving the instructions for the Queen's visit? I have it in mind that you will not go with us, Alice Burgin. I will not have the school shown up by such bad behaviour.'

Alice was mortified. Never in all her short life had she had her name called out in assembly and now she might not get to go to see the Queen. Her lip quivered uncontrollably and stinging tears welled in her eyes. It was all that Lily Sprawston's fault. While Miss Stanley had been going on about all the arrangements for the royal visit her friend Mary, who was sitting next to Alice, had been pointing at the nits crawling in the blond hair of the girl only a foot in front of their faces. Her mother had said to keep away from children with nits; she was fed up with them, so Alice had only shuffled back a few inches. But then you didn't get away with anything when eagle-eyed Miss Stanley was at the front, in her long grey dress and hair in a tight bun. Fortunately for Alice the head teacher on this occasion was willing to let it go at that, knowing quite well the effect that her sharp reprimand would have had on little Alice.

'You will be coming to school as normal on Friday morning,' continued Miss Stanley following the interruption, 'and after lunch we will be preparing to line up in class order. I will give out your green cards before we leave. You will only lose them if I give them out earlier! Your cards have a letter "G" on. This shows which division we are part of. You must take care of it because you will not be given your lemonade and bun following the singing without it. Our starting time is 2.25pm. The whole school will be marching up Duke Street to the top where we will join with the children from the nine other schools in our division. At 3pm. *precisely* we will all march to Norfolk Park, in columns eight abreast, girls first, the youngest leading, behind the Sheffield Temperance Band, and mind that you all have a clean white handkerchief and that you have polished your shoes. The Queen won't wish to be sung to by children with dirty shoes! Now, Mrs Briggs, if you could play for us I think that we will just run through the songs once more to make sure that everyone knows all the words. Let's start with the National Anthem. Stand up children.'

Alice loved singing. By the time that Miss Stanley had directed the whole school in the words and music of the four prescribed songs, the National Anthem, Diamond Reign, Llandaff and Rule Britannia, she was breathing more easily and her eyes and throat had almost stopped stinging.

'That was much better,' said Miss Stanley, 'although there are a few of the boys who are still not singing in tune. I think they will have to stand at the back and mime.' From the piano Mrs Briggs was making a waving sign towards the headmistress who stood on a low platform. 'Oh yes, Mrs Briggs is reminding me about the flags. The Duke of Norfolk, who you all know is our Mayor, has kindly presented each class with a Union Jack, which will be waved when Queen Victoria passes in her carriage. I have asked your teachers to choose one child from each class who has been specially good who will wave the class flag.' A quiet ripple of excitement ran through the tightly packed hall. The children filed out in silence back to their classrooms and at the end of the day Alice's teacher said, 'I have been thinking very carefully about whom I should choose to carry our class's Union Jack. It has been a very difficult decision but I have decided that it will be Lily Sprawston who is to have the honour of waving our flag.'

'Lily Sprawston! Nitty Lily! Waving our class flag.' Alice was nearly exploding with fury as she got out of the school gates and was walking home down Norwich Street. 'Well, I'm not cheering if Lily Sprawston's waving a flag!'

'Oh come on' replied Mary Proctor, her closest friend, 'let's go down to the sweet factory, I've got a penny. I don't care about Lily Sprawston anyway. I didn't want to wave any stupid flag.' Mary was a far more easy-going girl than Alice, who took everything to heart. She was already bouncing down the street playing hopscotch on the pattern of worn stone paving slabs, still wet and shining from the earlier rain. Things suddenly looked brighter. Of all the shops in Park the small stone-fronted shop in a terrace on Shrewsbury Road was every local child's favourite. Bypassing their own houses on Hague Lane they ran up South Street, past St Luke's Church, and by the time they reached the top the glorious odours of peppermint, aniseed and liquorice were mingling on the afternoon breeze with the usual smells of smoky Sheffield. Well, it wasn't Lily's fault that she had nits, thought Alice. After all, most of the children were infested at some time or other.

The sweet factory, was built facing up the steep bank, so, like many of the buildings in the Park, it had two storeys at the front and three at the rear. At the front it had one window divided into small square panes against which the girls' noses were now pressed. The smell of the sugar and spices boiling in the great shining copper vats, the clouds of pure white steam, which hung around the premises and the display in the window, had a mouth-watering effect. On white patterned doilies sat piles of the delicious confections, aniseed balls, lemon lozenges, liquorice comfits, mint rock and acid drops, ju-jubes and pastilles. Bottles of boiled sweets of every conceivable colour, shape and taste lined the narrow shelves. Alice and Mary made their decision and entered the door on the right. A tinkling bell summoned the shopkeeper from the door behind the heavy wooden counter, which filled most of the small shop, and he took up his usual position beside the polished brass scales.

'Can we have a ha'penny worth of fish, please?' asked Mary. The shopkeeper carefully took down the appropriate bottle, weighed out the brightly coloured fish-shaped sweets and slid them into a cone of paper. The sweets had a remarkable effect on raising Alice's spirits as the two girls dawdled home, sucking for all they were worth, and by the time Alice's sister got home and told the family the exciting news about the Queen's procession coming along Norfolk Road, she had all but forgotten Lily Sprawston and the unpleasant incident in assembly.

'Well, I don't know,' said their father, pushing back his chair, 'I think it's all a lot of fuss.'

'Oh George, how could you?' replied his wife.

'Well, you won't believe what's been going on at the factory. I've been taken off melting to paint! Everything that we can't move has been painted white and they've brought in tons of turf and plants and even trees in pots to go in the yard, and actually in the melting shop itself! You wouldn't believe it. It looks more like a market garden than a steel works! And to crown it all we've all got to wear these white jackets when she comes. I've never heard anything like it in my life.'

'Don't be so miserable dad,' said Emily, 'You know it's a great honour that the Queen is going to visit Cammell's. She could have chosen Firth's or John Brown's.'

'Aye, well, it was decided that she would come to Cammell's because of the orders for armour plating for the Navy's new ships. We are supposed to be working on orders for five at the present. They've got wonderful names: the *Ocean*, the *Glory*, the *Albion*, the *Goliath* and the *Canopus*, but it doesn't help when men are taken off to do other things, that's all I'm saying.' He knew that the argument was lost before he started for the whole town was in the grip of a royal frenzy ahead of the Queen's visit at the end of the week.

By the time that the day of the Queen's visit actually arrived Alice could hardly contain her excitement, which, truth to tell, had been caught by the rest of the family, including her father, although he would never admit it. As it had turned out they would all be involved in some way, father at the steel works, Alice in Norfolk Park, Emily on Norfolk Road and mother on the Moor where she was planning to go early to get a good position behind the barriers. Never had there been such preparations in the little house. The washing boiler had been steaming throughout Monday and Tuesday to ensure that the pinafores and aprons were spotless and on Thursday evening there was the entirely unprecedented event of the tin bath being brought in from the yard, placed in front of the fireplace and father, followed by the girls, having a bath—in the week! Emily carefully fashioned Alice's long dark hair into ringlets to which, in the morning, her mother added two new red bows. She put on her clean white pinafore, checked that her shoes were highly polished and that she had her clean handkerchief, and set off for school, knowing that it would be late before she returned home. Father and her sister had left the house long since.

It was a delightful morning, warm and sunny, 'The Queen's Weather', everyone said, for which she had a reputation. Along Norfolk Road the trees and gardens were at their late spring best. The great pear trees in the garden of Laithfield House looked as if they were weighed down with an icing-like fall of pure white snow and even from the house the bees could be heard humming and buzzing around the blossom. Most of the steel and cutlery works had declared it a holiday and so the town centre was already thronged with good-humoured early-morning visitors and workmen putting the final touches to the elaborate decorations and wooden stands in front of the town hall. Many couples enjoyed the novelty of promenading together whilst others drove along the route of the procession, passing beneath the triumphal arches that had been erected at intervals. On Pinstone Street, spanning the roadway near the Town Hall, stood a forty-foot high structure built in a classical theme from timber and plaster which bore the words 'Welcome to Victoria' across the top. Other arches had been erected in Commercial Street and in Barkers Pool. Fargate was lined with twenty-foot high Grecian columns connected across the road with garlands of foliage and fairy lights. Between these stood great pots with huge plant arrangements. The whole route from the Midland Station through the town was decorated with Venetian masts, flags, streamers, mottoes and floral garlands. There was much to admire and the time passed quickly. Never before or since has Sheffield celebrated as one in such style.

Towards noon the Kayes, leaving little Florence in the care of Emily, brought the carriage out of the carriage-house beside the drive, and harnessed the horse, which on a more usual day would be hauling the loaded wagon of fruit and vegetables with the lettering 'Enos Kaye' down the side that was so familiar on the streets of Sheffield. Enos, in his Sunday best, and Rebecca, parasol in hand, climbed into the carriage and they set off up Norfolk Road in the warm sunshine, one of his lads driving, beneath the simple floral arches which spanned it. Following the Queen's route in reverse, they drove through the gates and into Norfolk Park where the oak trees were in the freshest of new green foliage. The couple waved and Enos raised his new top hat to many of the friends and neighbours who were either sauntering

Laithfield House, little changed a century later

or driving around the carriage-drive. There was an infectious holiday mood in the air, which even old Mazeppa, named after a music hall act that they had seen at the Empire, seemed to catch as he cantered up the tree-lined avenue.

Down through the centre of the huge park was a vast natural amphitheatre from which the prospect down to the town centre and the hills beyond was glorious.

'Woah there boy,' called the lad, and the horse dutifully drew to a standstill at the top of the park so that the Kayes could watch the preparations for the children's arrival later in the day. An army of workmen were busy hauling miles of heavy rope to construct huge pens into which the fifty thousand children and two thousand teachers from the ninety-two Sheffield schools would be regimented. Down the centre a temporary road had been constructed along which the royal party would slowly pass between the massed ranks of children singing their long-rehearsed songs of praise to the Queen. Sounds of hammering and sawing came from the workmen constructing a huge wooden platform some thirty feet high from which the conductor, the famous Dr Henry Coward, would direct the massed choir and nine bands.

There were those who were sceptical about the wisdom of attempting to co-ordinate the singing and playing of such a massive assembly, the largest ever brought together, in the open air. Amongst them was Dr McNaught, the famous musical director from London, who was now surveying the preparations in the park with Dr Coward.

'What you are attempting here is simply not possible, Coward,' he said to the chorus master, 'the acoustics will have the effect of delaying the sound between the front and the rear of the assembly and it will be impossible to achieve a clear sound.'

'I think not, Dr McNaught. I have carefully considered the problem and I think that it will all work out excellently. You will see.'

'Well I do hope so my friend, or you will be left with considerable egg on your face! I must say, I do not share your confidence.'

Having driven down into the town and between the barriers along the Moor, the Kayes alighted in Barkers Pool and bid the lad return with the carriage immediately after the opening ceremony so that they could get up to the park in time to hear the singing. Already, despite it being only a little past two, there was an enormous throng of people round the Jubilee Monolith and in front of the Town Hall, and faces peered from the windows of all the offices that faced this way.

'Oh Enos, I told you that we should have got here earlier. All the best positions are already taken,' said Rebecca despairingly.

'Don't worry, my dear, I will make sure that we have a good view,' replied her husband, and sure enough, they had soon made their way towards the front of the file of people lining the barriers on Pinstone Street facing the Town Hall, from which the statue of the awaited personage stared down. There was plenty to entertain the good-natured crowd. Shortly before three the Boy's Brigade Band marched past and the police began to clear the roads of traffic. An orange-hawker with his cart, shouting 'Penny for two, all sweet!' was moved on and the man in fancy dress with a coat of mail who had paraded on his charger was evicted from the scene. A cheer went up as the whiskered veterans of the Crimean War marched past to take their position on the stand in front of the Crimean Monument, headed by their new banner, presented only the day before by Lady Mary Howard. The soldiers of the Hallamshire Rifles now marched up Fargate, eight hundred strong, and opened out in extended order to line the route right down the Moor and the famous Royal Highlanders, the Black Watch, took similar positions down Pinstone Street. Various military bands now accompanied the arrival of carriages bearing honoured guests who had been allocated seats on the grandstand. A cheer went up as the crowd recognised their MP, Mr Mundella, and soon Sir Howard Vincent, Sir Frederick Thorpe Mappin, Dr Sorby, Sir Henry Stevenson, Sir William Leng and many other notable local personalities joined him until, by four o'clock, a full hour before the expected arrival of the Royal train, the stands were full. Amongst the later arrivals had been the Duke and Duchess of Portland, Viscount and Viscountess Galway, the Earl of Wharncliffe, Earl Fitzwilliam and Lord and Lady Edmund Talbot. Somehow the orange-seller had managed to evade the cordon and now rode along the street on his cart, to the cheers of the crowd, a white ensign fluttering from a pole on his wagon. He was swiftly evicted.

Meanwhile, at The Farm, Henry Howard, the 15th Duke of Norfolk and hereditary Earl Marshal of England, was making the final preparations before himself setting off to the Town Hall to conduct the opening ceremonies.

'I do hope that all goes well,' he said to Lady Mary, his wife, as they settled themselves in the carriage, 'everyone has worked so hard to make today a day to remember.'

'I am quite sure that it will all go splendidly,' replied his wife distractedly. 'You must try not to worry. This is a big day for you and for Sheffield, and the people have you to thank for it. The Queen would not have considered accepting the invitation to open the Town Hall if it had not been for your being the Mayor. You know quite well that she takes little pleasure in such engagements these days, especially in the industrial north.' She was having a little trouble ensuring that the delicate purple material of her full dress was not creasing but having satisfied herself that all was well she adjusted her bonnet, composed of pink roses with small ostrich feathers, and the Duke gave the order for the coachman to proceed.

'Yes, I know my dear, and to have her make this visit to Sheffield in the year of her Diamond Jubilee makes this such a memorable occasion.' The Duke himself was, truth to tell, already feeling a little uncomfortably warm, which was not surprising as he was gorgeously dressed in his robes as Earl Marshal of England, with his heavy sword, over which he wore the magnificent red Mayoral cloak with its fur collar and chain of office and a tri-cornered hat with white plumes. In a short while the carriage was passing the front of the Midland Station and a cheer went up from the crowds assembled here. The Duke smiled, waved and began to relax a little, seeing that everything appeared to be well ordered. Coming up Norfolk Street they found themselves following the carriage of Earl Fitzwilliam. The coachman followed along Surrey Street and round to the front of the Town Hall, where they were greeted with a huge cheer.

There now ensued a moment of confusion for, on alighting from their carriage, the Duke and Duchess found that the way up the steps to the platform in front of the Town Hall gates was barred by a rope and that, even having somewhat inelegantly ducked beneath it, the gates were closed and they were shut out! It was quickly pointed out, however, that the coachman had made a mistake and that they should have met the party, who were gathering to meet the Queen at the station, at the Surrey Street entrance, so they retook their seats and, following this embarrassing incident, were driven to the correct location.

At Park Board School Alice's class teacher was calling the register. 'Lily Sprawston.' No answer. 'Where is Lily Sprawston?' Mary's hand shot up.

'Please miss, Lily's mother says to tell you that she's got scarlet fever.'

'Oh no, not today,' retorted the teacher. 'Well, we will just have to choose someone else to carry the flag won't we? Let me look at you all. Now show me your handkerchiefs.'

The children dutifully held out their handkerchiefs. Some were crisp and new but many of the crumpled pieces of dirty cloth grudgingly presented for inspection by various boys clearly put them out of the running. One or two were trying to disguise the fact that they had not got one. 'Jack Marriott, where is your handkerchief? Show it to me this instant.'

'I a'nt got one miss,' he mumbled.

'If you want to go with the rest of the children to sing for the Queen you had better make sure that you have one by this afternoon, Jack Marriott, or Miss Stanley will send you home. Now I will come round and inspect your shoes. Stand to the side, children.'

This is where most of the boys and some girls came unstuck. Shoes were always a problem. They had all seen better days, having been repaired many times and handed down from elder brothers and sisters. Kicking things around the street on the way to school had taken a toll on some. Fortunately for Alice her mother had managed to save up and had bought her a new pair for last Whit Monday's walk. She stood up as smartly as she could, her pinafore fresh and clean and her ringlets bobbing and hoped that she would be picked.

'Yes, I think that I will choose Alice Burgin to carry the flag now that poor Lily is ill. She looks so smart that she will be a credit to our class.'

Alice beamed with pleasure and looked across to Mary who returned her wide grin.

'Now, sit down. I am going to give out your green card and your medal that the Mayor has presented you with so that you will always remember this special day. You are to use the safety pin to pin it securely onto your jacket or dress.' Alice held in her hand the light grey coloured medallion and she knew that she would always treasure it.

'We will read out the words together children,' said the teacher when all the medallions had been distributed. *In Commemoration of the Loving Welcome given by the Children of Sheffield to Queen Victoria in Norfolk Park, May, 1897. 1837 to 1897 Diamond Jubilee,* the class intoned, some with more sureness than others.

At 2.35pm precisely the ranks of 1,240 children from Park Board School set off to march up Duke Street to meet with the 4,500 children from the other schools in the area to swell the massive assembly in Norfolk Park. There could have been none prouder than little Alice Burgin as she marched along on the outside of the eight-deep rank holding high the staff with the Union Jack which fluttered in the light spring breeze.

On The Moor, then called South Street, where Alice's mother had found a suitable position behind the barrier, the street vendors were having a veritable field day. 'Remember the li'l 'uns at 'oam,' shouted the man in the overcoat selling cheap penny toys. Another, with fancy balloons for sale shouted, 'Who'll buy a baby? Jubilee babies a penny.' Particularly good sellers were the programmes of the visit printed on Japanese handkerchiefs, and the different designs of commemorative medals. All in all, it reminded her of a day at Sheffield fair, especially when the strains of 'Tommy Atkins' and 'The Death of Nelson' drifted down from the band of the Dannemora Steel Works who were positioned beneath the Crimea Monument. Near the bottom of the long street, where the procession was due to pass along one of the less salubrious quarters of he town, mainly occupied by rough grinders and buffers, along Hereford Street, the crowd grew less polite and, as people vied for better vantage places, scuffles and fights broke out in the long hot afternoon, though these were soon quelled by the police. A cheer went up as a column of children passed along the road on their long march from their schools in Crookes, Ranmoor and Fulwood to Norfolk Park.

On Norfolk Road, Emily was out walking baby Florence in her perambulator. All through the afternoon there had been a constant procession of people making their way towards the Park, including streams of weary-looking children. A contingent of soldiers from the Royal Artillery marched up and took position at the South Street end, whilst a similar contingent from the Robin Hood Rifles were stationed at the Park entrance. Already the sounds of brass bands drifted down the road. Some of the spectators, weary in the unforeseen heat, settled themselves behind the barriers on Norfolk Road, and on one occasion one of the passing children fell out of step, faltered and fainted, almost in front of Emily. She rushed forwards to give assistance, but the teacher was quickly there to give reassurance and a reviving drink from a flask. By four o'clock all the massed choir was due to be assembled but it was, in fact, almost three-quarters of an hour later that the last schools were wearily taking their places. For Alice and her friends the long wait, crammed behind the barriers on the warm grass, seemed interminable and they were pleased when, under the direction of Dr Coward, the bands struck up and they began to practise their songs.

'Loyal and loving the children now raising, Welcoming voices in joyous refrain.' The words and tune, now so familiar to Emily, came drifting down the road as fifty thousand little voices struck up 'Diamond Reign.' The sound sent shivers right down her spine. 'Listen Florence,' she said to the baby, 'that's our Alice singing.'

It was nearing five o'clock, the appointed time for the arrival of the Royal train and the whole of Sheffield held its breath in anticipation. As Emily stood rocking Florence in the afternoon sunshine outside Laithfield House, she was startled by a sudden loud crack of artillery fire. It was the salute from the soldiers on the Hyde Park Parade Ground nearby to announce the arrival of the train bearing the first reigning monarch ever to visit the town. The sound echoed through the town and around the surrounding hills and a flutter of excitement ran through the eager crowds in front of the Town Hall for within fifteen minutes the Queen of England, Victoria herself, would draw up in front of them.

Dressed, as usual, all in black, relieved only by the glitter of jet on a small velvet mantle and a few tips of white ostrich feathers in her bonnet, Queen Victoria was assisted out of the carriage and across the red carpet beneath the specially erected canopy on the station platform. Henry Howard, the Duke of Norfolk and soon to be Sheffield's first Lord Mayor, bowed and greeted her. They passed a few friendly words before she climbed into the open carriage which stood only a few steps away. Her daughter, Princess Christian and son, the Duke of Connaught, magnificently decked in full military uniform and sporting a full waxed moustache, accompanied the Queen. The procession of carriages formed up behind the mounted police, including the Chief Constable, John Jackson, and set off at a brisk pace between the cheering throng. In only a few minutes Rebecca and Enos Kaye, waiting at the Town Hall, caught the faint sound of cheering and began to crane their necks to get a first glimpse of the proceedings. Then everything seemed to happen all at once. The Chief Constable was cheered as the police trotted up Fargate and round the corner, followed by the Royal Lancers, pennons flying. The carriages of the Duke and Duchess and the Aldermen drew up at the steps and they took their places in front of the closed gates. When the Queen's carriage at last appeared everyone was so eager to take away an impression of the scene that they would always remember that the huge crowd fell unexpectedly quiet.

The carriage was brought to a standstill in front of the waiting dignitaries and the Duke stepped forward to begin the official ceremonies, the formal addresses and presentations, during which the Queen, who did not alight from the carriage now or indeed at any point of the two-hour visit to the city, cast her veiled gaze up to admire the splendour of the grand new building; the gilt gateway, the allegorical figures flanking the doorway and the frieze of craftsmen, the figures of Thor and Vulcan and, a little above this, the figure of herself in contrasting white stone. All, she remarked to the Duke was simply splendid.

Then, following the line of the tower upwards, Queen Victoria's eyes fell on the figure standing on the topmost pinnacle, high above the building, a bronze figure holding high a sheaf of arrows glinting in the late afternoon sun. She squinted a little, trying to make out its features before quickly averting her gaze and frowning slightly. Can this be correct, she thought. Have the people of Sheffield really erected the statue of a naked man on top of their Town Hall? She would have to take this up with the Duke!

By now the Queen was being handed a brass box from which a key protruded. 'If your Majesty would do us the honour of turning the key,' said Alderman Langley MP, 'the gates will open.' The Queen took pleasure in performing the little ceremony, and, with a fanfare of trumpets and a huge cheer the gates slid smoothly open. Little did the old Queen know, however, but this was not one of the mechanical feats of the modern world. The turning of the key simply lit a light bulb behind the doors that was the signal to the two workmen hidden there to pull on the ropes which were attached to the gates. One or two of the councillors on the platform looked across at each other and smiled knowingly.

The formal proceedings were now at an end and as the bands played the procession formed up and began to proceed down Pinstone Street. Rebecca waved and cheered as the Royal carriage passed and the Queen turned and gave a graceful wave which she was sure was meant just for her. As the last of the carriages passed under the great arch and on down The Moor the massed crowds that had witnessed the formal ceremony were already beginning to break up. It soon became apparent that the Kaye's original plan would be impossible.

'Enos, look at these crowds. The lad will not be able to get back with the carriage through all this. We shall miss seeing the procession as it comes along our road,' said Rebecca. 'Shall we walk?'

'I think we had better. As you say there is no chance of getting back in time if we don't. It's not far.'

Fortunately, many people were of the same mind so the throng of people was drawn down Fargate, High Street and Commercial Street, from where it was but a short step to the bottom of South Street down which the Royal procession would pass on its route to the Cyclops works.

Alice's mother, standing near the top of Matilda Street, was in an excellent position to see the full length of the long-awaited procession as it passed beneath the great white-plastered arch and proceeded, amidst great cheering and waving of flags, slowly towards her. The people of Sheffield were familiar with processions down The Moor, for the long straight road provided the perfect setting for such spectacles as the annual Lifeboat Day Parades or the parade of Sanger's Circus, complete with elephants and snarling lions. Never before, however, had the street witnessed a parade of such splendour. The music, the uniforms, the fine horses and the dignitaries, all made a lasting impression, to say nothing of the climax, the sight of the Queen of England, Victoria herself, driving past, smiling and waving. When the procession had passed, Alice's mother turned and was swept along with the throng making its way to Park Hill, down Matilda Street.

In Norfolk Park Dr Coward instructed the bugler to sound. It now became clear how he proposed to keep control of the enormous assembly; standing on the high rostrum he raised his arms and every child and bandsman could clearly see that he held a six-foot-long white baton to the end of which a white flag was attached. The band struck up and the strains of 'Diamond Reign' swelled from fifty thousand voices. It was 6.15pm before the Queen's carriage finally swept through the Belle View gates at the bottom of the park and drew up beside the conductor's rostrum. The colossal cheer that accompanied her arrival must have been audible far across the city below.

'Your Majesty, may I have the honour of presenting to you the children of Sheffield,' said the Duke of Norfolk. The Queen looked round at the extraordinary sea of young faces and smiled. 'Indeed, what a wonderful reception,' replied the Queen. And now was the moment that the children had so long prepared for. The conductor raised his long baton and the children's mouths opened wide in unison with the patriotic words of the song. *Blessings of Fatherland richly are falling, Crowning the ripening years that remain,* they sang, every word clear and precise. The effect was dramatic. One of the guard of honour, a sergeant who stood in front of the pen near Alice, looked as though he was clearly in great discomfort, struggling to retain his composure. 'Are you alright?' asked the teacher, as tears began to stream down his face. 'Yes, ma'am' he replied. 'Who can help blubbing when you see a sight like that,' for the old Queen herself had clearly been similarly moved to tears. As the song ended Dr McNaught, who had been standing beside the rostrum, shouted up, 'Bravo Coward. You have quite upset all my careful calculations of how it could not be done!'

Of this momentous gathering there was to be, unfortunately, virtually no good photographic record. The professional photographer who was to perform the commission had taken six plates of the assembled crowds from the top of the conductor's stand and then waited until the Queen drew up before

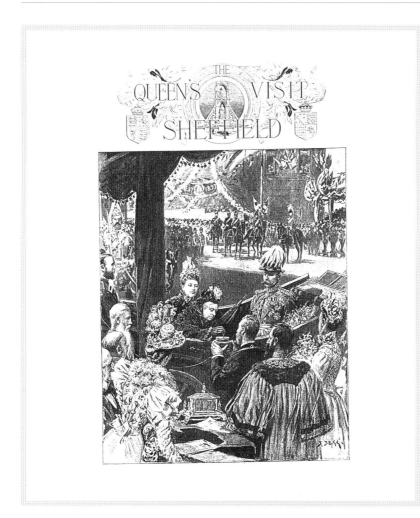

hastily exposing another six. Unfortunately on returning to his darkroom to develop the plates he found to his horror that the first six were very over-exposed and obscure and the second six blank. In his haste he had exposed the same plates twice!

Amidst the rousing strains of 'Rule Britannia' the carriages then moved off, sweeping up in front of Alice and through the massed choir to the top of the park. The procession then swung round and drove at a brisk pace down the carriage-road and out of the Norfolk Road gates. Alice, with her friends, all holding tightly onto their precious green cards, were shepherded to their refreshment booth where they were met by the welcome sight of a mountain of buns and gallons of lemonade in jugs. Here she had been instructed to wait until her mother arrived to collect her. 'Stay where I can find you,' her mother had instructed, 'and whatever you do, don't go into Cherry Wood.' She did not need telling twice. Nobody went into the bit of gloomy woodland at the top of the park. Everyone knew that if you did, Spring-Heeled Jack would get you.

In front of Laithfied House Emily watched as the first of the carriages bearing the Duke and Duchess emerged through the gothic gates of the park and headed down Norfolk Road towards where she and little Florence waited with a group of maids and servants in their starched white caps and aprons from nearby houses. At that point Rebecca and Enos Kaye joined them, having walked from town, and they stood together cheering as the cavalcade trotted past, rather more quickly than Emily would have liked, on its way past the Cholera Monument and the Shrewsbury Hospital, down towards Charles Cammell's steel works.

South Street, down which it now turned, bore quite a different aspect for here the hill was lined not with gentlemen and ladies in their fashionable best, or even by maids and servants, but by the local grinders, cutlers and forgers who had left off their work at the wheel and workbench only a little time before. Indeed, in this neighbourhood there had been no signs of a general holiday and little stir until at least four o'clock when the first of the craftsmen, in their caps, thick waistcoats, shirtsleeves and scarves, began to congregate beside the road with their aproned wives. Those folk who had joined the onlookers here, having already witnessed the ceremony at the Town Hall, had to take a back position. The street was now packed and a stray grinder's dog, clearly spooked by the proceedings, was cheered raucously as it ran the whole length of the street as if in a race!

'Let's give t'Duke a good 'en, lads,' shouted a thick-set grinder as the first military outriders rounded the top corner, and a rousing cheer went up as the Duke's carriage appeared, followed by the other conveyances including that of the Queen's party, and continued down the hill. And so it was all the way along the thickly lined streets as the company proceeded over the river and down Saville Street towards the gates of the Cyclops Steel Works. Not everything, unfortunately, went without mishap. Whilst the crowds who had gathered on Blonk Street Bridge cheered the passing Royal procession, John Rodgers, a labourer who had climbed up onto the parapet to get a better view, overbalanced and fell into the shallow river Don below where his friends watched him struggling. A seaman, who happened to be nearby, made the perilous jump into the river and swam around looking for the man who had now disappeared. It was not until the next morning that his body was discovered when the river was dragged.

Alice's father, skilled at judging by eye the temperature of the great steel ingot in the reheating furnace by its exact colour, had watched from his position beside the heavy furnace door as the wooden stands facing it had filled with the dignitaries who had come to witness one of the greatest spectacles the city had to offer, the rolling of a steel plate. All the worthies who had been at the opening ceremony had now taken their places awaiting the arrival of the Queen. Amongst them sat Charles Cammell and his wife. At last the Queen's carriage turned into the works and passed through what would be called hereafter the Royal Entrance and beneath the archway from which hung a great painting of a battleship at sea. The entrance way and the great shed had been transformed by the grass, trees and plants that now lined it. Once the Royal carriage had been drawn inside the works the Royal Lancers formed up in a semi-circle at the gate and hundreds of the factory's 10,000 workers poured into the roadway behind them.

Alice's father watched as the Duke and the Lord Chamberlain came forward to the Queen's carriage and presented her and the Princess with hand-held screens of darkened glass which were mounted in gold and tortoiseshell to protect their eyes from the glare when the furnace door opened and the almost white-hot ingot weighing thirty-three tons was revealed. The signal was given to the team and the great door was raised and a huge pair of pincers, operated by a crane, was manipulated into position to grab the ingot and steadily draw it from the mouth of the oven onto an iron carriage. The team, Alice's father amongst them, worked with their usual precision, coaxing and heaving the white-hot ingot into position and bringing the carriage up to the rollers using long steel bars as levers. The process of rolling the ingot backwards and forwards between the massive rollers was accompanied by loud rumblings and clanging and, as one of the workmen standing closely threw bundles of birch twigs onto the hot ingot as it passed through the rollers, a process which helped to remove the scale, the whole thing flared, hissed and spat alarmingly. Alice's father was far too engrossed in this dangerous process to notice that the Queen, in spite of the screen, was finding the heat and the noise overwhelming. A signal was given to the leading roller in the team and the procedure was halted. It was time for the Queen to leave. Victoria gave a slight nod to the team of men as the carriage turned, passed through the gate and headed back down Saville Street towards the station. At a little after 7 pm the party boarded the Royal train and it carried on its northward journey, taking the Queen to Balmoral. The visit had lasted precisely two hours.

Later, at The Farm, Henry Howard, the 15th Duke of Norfolk, and now the first Lord Mayor of the newly incorporated City of Sheffield, breathed a heavy sigh of relief. 'Well, I think that it all went well my dear,' he said to his wife.

'It all went splendidly. The Queen herself said so, and you know that her majesty would not say that unless she had been truly impressed.'

'No, I know,' replied the Duke, walking over to the window. 'I think she was rather overwhelmed at the steel works, but I don't think that she will quickly forget the children's singing.' The vast garden was looking its best. He took in the broad banks of rhododendrons, now in full flower beside the lake, the lawns and the sweep of Clay Wood behind. His attention was drawn to the monument that crowned the wooded hill. The elegant honey-coloured stone shaft seemed to glow in the last of the day's sun. He smiled again as he recalled the singing in the park. 'What a day!' he said, almost to himself, 'What a day!'

The following day a telegram arrived addressed to the Duke. He realised at once that it had come from the Queen. She had written: *Safely arrived here. I wish again to express my great gratification at the very loyal and hearty reception I met with yesterday at Sheffield. I wish also to say how much I admired the children's' singing and the admirable way in which everything was arranged.*

THE DIVIDED COMMUNITY

Sheffield has always displayed deep social divisions and the developments on Park Hill starkly reflected this. At the same time as the workers' families were struggling to live in such poor conditions at the foot of the hill, elegant stone-built villas with carriage houses and stables were being built further up the hill for those who could afford to get out of the smoke. This is today's Norfolk Road, with its squarely-built detached houses of honey-coloured stone which were built in the years following the interments nearby in the Cholera Burial Grounds. It has been engulfed by less elegant developments but even today retains an air of faded gentility and calm, only a stone's throw from the city centre bustle. On the steeper western-facing hillside overlooking the Sheaf Valley even grander estates were being laid out

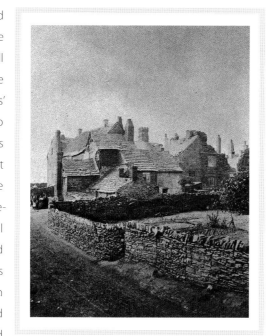

Around the ruins of Manor Lodge
a strange little hamlet developed

for the industrial elite of the town: Queen's Tower, built for the silversmith Samuel Roberts, which still stands, and The Farm, built for the Dukes of Norfolk, which does not. The stone lodges at the gates of these properties are still a feature of East Bank. For these privileged few, the 13th Duke landscaped a green space from a piece of reclaimed industrial land and laid it out with fine tree-lined avenues and promenades. Here, in what became known as Norfolk Park, the well-to-do could take the air as they rode round the carriage drives or listened to the band on a Sunday afternoon.

Beyond this the fields and farmland, dotted with stone-built farmhouses and cottages and the occasional headstocks of one of the Duke's mines, stretched uninterrupted to the top of Park Hill. Only around the ruins of the Tudor Manor Lodge itself did a strange little hamlet develop. Here, within the very ruins of the venerable building which, like most of Sheffield's ancient buildings, was looted for building stone, there grew up a small-scale industrial community. Part of the Great Kitchen wing adjoining Manor Lane became a public house and brewery, a potter of some distinction named John Fox established his kiln in the great tower in which Wolsey had been royally entertained, extensive farm buildings occupied the hillside just beneath the site and a colliery was sunk in the former outer court. A range of ramshackle workers' cottages clung, limpet-like, to the ruins of the long gallery and others were built along Manor Lane. To minister to their spiritual needs, a chapel was built, presided over in the nineteenth century by the charismatic William Cowlishaw, known as 'Praying William', who had undergone a life-changing conversion from the dissipated ways of his youth. The Cowlishaws still live in the area having occupied one of the cottages until they were demolished in the 1970s.

Throughout the nineteenth century the successive Dukes paid intermittent personal interest to the town.

THE LATE WILLIAM COWLISHAW.

The 12th Duke built a new house called Beech Hill on Norfolk Park Road for his agent Michael Ellison in 1819 and the 14th Duke rebuilt 'The Farm' and spent some part of each year in the town. It was not until the end of the Victorian era, however, that the close association which Duke Henry, the 15th Duke, established with the city was to bring to a climax the relationship between the Howards and Sheffield. Duke Henry came to the title in 1860. His dukedom therefore coincided with the period of Sheffield's greatest economic prosperity, when the vast East End steelworks of the lower Don Valley were pre-eminent in the world. The Duke served as Mayor and the city's first Lord Mayor and it was at his invitation that Queen Victoria, no great lover of the industrial north, agreed to open the Town Hall on May 21st, 1897. He had the honour to be the first Freeman of the city and gave the City its ceremonial mace and chain. He played a leading part in the establishment of the University of Sheffield and was awarded its first honorary degree. He rebuilt the Corn Exchange, where the Park roundabout now stands, in splendid gothic style, and

Norfolk Heritage Park

did much to enhance the appearance of the city centre.

It is Duke Henry that we have to thank for most of the surviving historical features of the Norfolk Trail. It is he who recognised the importance of the Turret House at the Manor Lodge, rescued it from oblivion and had it very carefully restored to its original condition. He was also responsible for the restoration of the Shrewsbury Chapel in the Cathedral, with its spectacular memorials to his Tudor ancestors. In addition he gave to the people of the city recreation gardens and parks to the value of £150,000, the greatest single gift being that of Norfolk Park itself, which he bequeathed to the City in May 1909. It is perhaps fitting that one of the very few full-scale statues to Sheffield worthies is the superb figure of the 15th Duke of Norfolk that sits on the grand staircase in the entrance hall of his great town hall.

IN THIS GARDEN
134 CITIZENS REST
IN A COMMUNAL
✙ GRAVE ✙
THEIR NAMES
ARE RECORDED
THEY DIED BY ENEMY ACTION
✙

MARY DYSON, now 95 years old, was brought up in Number 2, Court 6, Duke Street, the site of which is now covered by the Park Square roundabout. In this tiny courtyard cottage of just three rooms, one downstairs and two tiny bedrooms, she lived as a child with her parents, two brothers and three sisters. All six children shared one tiny bedroom, the girls in the big bed that took up most of the room and the boys in a crib. As they got bigger there was so little room that they had to take turns to dress. She recalls without affection the squalor of those living conditions when, every Friday, all the occupants of the six cottages around the yard would move all their furniture and possessions into the middle of the court so that they could give the lodgings a thorough clean to rid the house and furniture of the lice and vermin with which it was infested. It was a joyless upbringing; her father, a carter at the fruit market, was remote, taking all his meals by himself and only seldom communicating with his family. She never remembers him showing any affection towards any of the family, and, when at the age of twelve she qualified for a place at the High School, he refused point blank to entertain the idea, telling her that he 'wasn't having any of his family getting ideas above their station', and that was the end of her schooling. It was not until Mary was eighteen years old that their living conditions slightly improved. At this stage the family, now desperate for space and having three wage-earners in the family, were able to scrape together the increased rent of 13/- a week, a big increase from the 6/- they had been paying to the Duke of Norfolk, and move to a slightly more commodious accommodation just round the corner in South Street.

Sheffield, it is often said, is a city composed of village communities, and nowhere was this more apparent than Park Hill. As in the eighteenth century the community looked to itself. The children found their entertainment in the maze of courtyards and jennels, the more

Mary Dyson

enterprising girls putting on 'shows' mounted on the dustbins. They did not venture far; it got 'posh' if you went beyond Robinson Road, higher up the hill. The centre of early social life was the Chapel; Mary attended the nearby Park Weslyan Chapel and played the kettledrums in the Girls Brigade Band. Later she became a Sunday School Teacher. All the children attended the same school, Park Board School, which opened in 1874 between Lord Street and Duke Street Lane to replace the earlier National School. In such a confined world events such as marching in procession behind the banner to the annual Whit

Sing in Norfolk Park were major highlights in the year, especially as this was the only time of the year that you got any new clothes.

The many public houses in the Park provided the focus for the men's entertainment so it is not surprising that the brass bands of the Band of Hope and the Salvation Army regularly paraded the streets. Mary signed the pledge at the age of seven! As the girls and boys grew up, the cinemas began to take the place of the Sunday School. Mary lived opposite the Park Picture House on South Street. It cost a penny to get in but if she carried her brother Bill on her back and her sister Violet carried Lilly on hers they could save tuppence to spend on sweets. The seats were wooden benches and a burly attendant, nicknamed 'Elmo The Mighty', would poke them with a stick to make them move up. Here the silent films were accompanied by a tinkling piano but, if the girls had enough money, they would pay the extra tuppence to go to the Norfolk, where there was also a violinist! It was to the pictures that Mary's young man, Sydney Dyson, would take her before they were married. Later they would become activists in the Labour party, Mary becoming Sheffield's Lady Mayoress when Sydney was Lord Mayor in the early 1970s.

At the same time, for the children of the far smaller number of well-to-do families who lived half a mile up the hill on Norfolk Road, life could not have been more different. Elizabeth Crowther, generally known as 'Bessie' was born in 1912 at Laithfield House, 64, Norfolk Road, and experienced what she is only too willing to admit was a sheltered and privileged upbringing. The house itself had ample space, with a breakfast room, lounge and dining room as well as the kitchen and scullery. On the top floor was a garret, reached by a narrow back staircase from the kitchen, which accommodated one of the maids. The semi-detached house was set in its own well-tended gardens with stabling for two horses and a carriage-house. Here, and in Clay Wood, which was reached through an opening in the garden wall, Bessie and her two brothers were in a world of their own and needed nothing more for their amusement. Brought up by a governess until she was seven years old, Bessie was then sent to be educated at a girl's school in Broomhill. On a Sunday the Crowthers would attend the morning service at the Cathedral and here the boys joined the scouts. The family was musical and evenings were spent with friends and

Mary Hannah and Edwin Crowther, with their three children, Geoffrey, Edwin and Bessie. Photographed c.1914

neighbours round the piano. Mother played the piano and father, who by day was a company secretary at a steel works, played violin and cello. Everyone joined in the parlour songs whilst little Bessie, put to bed at six, crept to the landing to listen through the banisters, entranced. From these earliest days she developed such a love of music that she has spent her life as a piano teacher and still plays beautifully at over ninety.

To the Crowthers, however, as to so many Sheffield families, the night of the Blitz, December 12th 1940, was an event of such dramatic intensity that their lives were never the same afterwards. There had been minor raids before this but on this night of still-remembered terror the dull thuds and tremors began in the early evening and continued right through the night whilst the frightened family huddled in terror on the cellar steps. They were lucky. Their uncle's house next door had every window blown out by the enormous explosion of a bomb that landed in the nearby woods but at number 64 the only damage was to the roof, which was not discovered until later when water began to pour through. The parents, however, decided to move the family out and they were dispersed between a friend's farm near Pontefract and Doncaster. The house was sold shortly afterwards, both parents died and a whole way of life had come to an end.

George Haywood was four when the First World War ended, his earliest recollection being of sitting on the pavement outside the house in the lower Park watching heavy horses with soldiers on their backs hauling gun carriages up St John's Road towards Hyde Park Barracks. As for many a Park lad, a harsh upbringing forced him to live on his wits and become something of a chancer. The children were always hungry. The meagre wages earned in a local pit by their father didn't stretch to providing much more than bread and dripping for the hungry family during the week. Clothes, bought annually through his mother's saving in the tuppence ha'penny club, were soon in holes and his boots patched with cardboard but since most people were in the same position there was no disgrace in accepting handouts from charity.

George missed more school than he attended and by the age of twelve was earning what he could by doing odd jobs such as portering at the Victoria Station or hawking fruit from the wholesale market around Handsworth and Swallownest. One momentous day, however, an ambulance drew up at the door and his father was stretchered in, his leg smashed in an accident at the pit. With little coming in there was not much that his parents could do to make ends meet and so they turned to George and asked him if he would take father's place at the pit. He felt there was little choice. He was just fourteen years old. To begin with he earned about 38p a week leading the ponies to the coalface and back to the shaft bottom. He enjoyed the companionship of the pit and was soon drawn into the prevailing gang culture that was then at its violent height. As a member of 'The Park Lads' he was always fighting and getting chased home through the alleys by the police. Members of the Mooney Gang lived on nearby

Bernard Street and ran the local gambling ring. There were times when mounted police would come galloping up Chancel Street onto the hills behind George's house in an attempt to catch the gamblers at the tossing ring. They were rarely successful in the early days, though following the execution of the Fowler brothers for murder things quietened considerably.

By the age of eighteen George was married but was still doing odd jobs to earn extra money, including scrap dealing and asphalting. By now he had progressed in the pit to blasting and it was then that he suffered the inevitable accidents. In the first a roof-fall resulted in the loss of three fingers and in the second a piece of rock shattered his leg. He was too shocked to continue work in the mine but since this was the second year of the war, he was forced to stand in front of a tribunal of five judges who decided that he should go back. George made it quite clear that if forced back to the pit he would kill himself and so they relented and he was sent to work on another reserved occupation on a forging hammer at Firth Brown Steels, like so many other Park Hill men.

In the early years of the 20th century most of the area of the ancient Park was still agricultural and semi-rural in nature. When Prince of Wales Road was laid out in 1921, following the eastern edge of the Park, it snaked across open country. The farmsteads which had been built in the early eighteenth century, Manor Oaks, Arbourthorne and Wybourn Farms, still dotted the landscape. During the inter-war years, however, the fields and farmland stretching from the Manor to Intake were finally swallowed up by the geometrically-planned development of the Manor housing estate, the lower slopes facing the Don Valley to the north were developed as the Wybourn Estate and the vast area of the Arbourthorne Estate was complete by 1939. These estates provided new homes for hundreds of families moved from older

Aerial view of the Manor area: mid-20th century

areas of the city under clearance orders. Unfortunately however, the City Council had only just begun to get to grips with ridding lower Park Hill of its scandalous slum dwellings when the Second World War broke out. By this time the area had acquired for itself an unenviable reputation for crime and gang warfare

Unemployment was rife and to some gambling suggested a last vestige of hope. During the 1920s Skye Edge became one of Sheffield's principal venues for an illegal 'tossing ring' that flourished there. Control of this lucrative venture was jealously guarded, and gangs under the control of notorious characters like George Mooney and Sam Garvin who did not hesitate to use extreme violence to assert their rival claims. The police response that finally brought the gangs to heel used similarly uncompromising techniques.

$\mathcal{L}$OOKING $\mathcal{B}$ACK

November 1ˢᵗ 2003

'I'LL BRING YOU A CUP OF TEA in bed this morning if you like. You stay there, you still look a bit pale. I don't really know what it was that you saw that gave you such a fright but it wasn't like you to get so upset.' Margaret's husband, Brian, was all concern this morning, trying to make up to her for his behaviour the previous night when he had been so impatient with her.

'It's alright. You needn't bother,' replied Margaret, still a little short with him and now somewhat embarrassed by her behaviour. 'I'm getting up now. I've got things to do. Where's Charlotte? We are going down to Gran's to help her make a start on the packing. She's got to be out of Park Hill in a few weeks and you know how it's worrying her.'

Charlotte had already had her breakfast and was ready to be off.

'You are up and about early this morning,' said her mum coming down the stairs, 'What's all this about?'

'It's just that we've been given this work to do by Mrs Briggs at school. We're doing this work in history about the Second World War and she says we have got to talk to an old person about what it was like. I thought I could talk to Granny Velma this morning.'

'Oh dear, don't you start her talking about the past for goodness sake,' laughed her mother, 'or we'll never get away! Ryan, are you coming with us to Gran's or are you going to behave yourself if I leave you here?'

Ryan was nine and generally trustworthy.

'I want to finish this game on my computer' shouted Ryan down the stairs.

'Alright, but behave yourself,' added mum, as she and Charlotte left the house.

It did not take them long to drive the short distance down to Gran, who lived in one of the flats on Long Henry Row, high on the Park Hill block. Charlotte always enjoyed visiting grandma Velma, who claimed her mother took her unusual name from the wrapper on a bar of Czechoslovakian chocolate.

She loved to stand on the little balcony and look over the amazing scene of the busy city centre spread out in front of her, and her granny was such a character. 'Come in,' she said, opening the door to them, 'I have to keep it locked. You never know who is coming and going along this balcony. There was such a row out here last night, people shouting and swearing. I don't know what it was all about.'

'I shall be glad when you've moved off here, mother,' said Margaret, following her into the over-crowded room.

'Oh, I'm right enough, don't you worry,' replied her mother as she took off the lid from her battered old tin and passed a Penguin biscuit to Charlotte. It was a familiar routine. 'I hope I can get one of the flats back on here when they have been done up, it used to be so nice when they were first built you know.'

'Have you lived here all that time?' asked Charlotte, thinking already about Mrs Briggs and her project.

'Aye, I have that, and I can tell you it was like coming to a palace.'

'Why, where did you live before, Gran.'

'I lived on Greystock Street, down Attercliffe. We didn't realise it till we come here but it was no better than a slum. There were just a toilet in the yard that we all had a key to and at the back there were pigsties. I can still remember the terrible smell when they cooked up the swill on a Friday to feed them for the week. We only had one room downstairs, one upstairs and an attic. There was no gas, my mother had to cook everything on the open fire and that was the only heat in the house. When we went to bed in winter we took a warm dinner plate to warm the bed.

'That sounds terrible, Gran!'

'Well, it was not so bad really. We didn't know any different and we had some happy times. People seemed more friendly then, somehow. We never needed to lock the door you know. We never had any money though. Every Monday I was sent down to the pawn shop to pawn my father's trousers,' she laughed, 'I had to watch out first to check that there was nobody in the street that we knew. I got 5/- and I had to collect them again on a Friday ready for the weekend.'

'Yes, come on now. I haven't come to spend my weekend listening to your old stories again,' said Margaret. 'Charlotte, if you want hear more you will have to come yourself and talk to Gran.'

Charlotte hurriedly finished jotting all this down in her little notebook, pushed it into her bag and began to help her mum to wrap the dozens of ornaments in newspaper and pack them into cardboard boxes. Granny Velma, however, kept an eagle eye on the proceedings lest any of her precious belongings be damaged, regretting that arthritis in her hands prevented her from doing the job herself.

'Really mother, I don't know what you want to keep all this stuff for, I really don't. You only have to clean it.' But to Charlotte, whose mother wouldn't have 'junk' in the house, every piece was a treasure.

'You'll never guess what happened last night, Grandma,' said Charlotte, 'Mum had a right fright. She says she saw Spring-Heeled Jack.'

'I'm not surprised,' replied Velma as she wandered into the kitchen to make a pot of tea, 'I was always telling her he'd come for her one day when she was being a naughty girl.'

'Mother!' exclaimed Margaret. 'Its no wonder I grew up thinking I see things is it, when you used to fill my head with such nonsense.'

Charlotte laughed as she pulled out the second drawer of the sideboard and came across an old flat cardboard box with roses on the top. She carefully lifted the lid and found real treasure; black and white photographs, faded and dog-eared, but none the less fascinating. Most of them were of faces. She sat down with the box on her knee and began to leaf through them as Velma came back.

'Who are these?' asked Charlotte, picking out a sepia-coloured picture of a group of girls in long overalls and headscarves.

'Oh, that's me, there in the middle. I can remember now when that was taken. I'd just started work at Taylor's Eye Witness Works on Milton Street.'

She pointed out a pretty young girl with a shy smile, looking little older than her granddaughter herself.

'What did you do there, Gran?'

'I was a buffer girl, duck. We used to have to polish all the spoons and forks, and a mucky job is was too. I worked there over thirty years.'

'Can I borrow this to show my teacher?' asked Charlotte.

'Yes, of course you can. I want it back mind. I know what your mother is for chucking stuff out,' added Velma, casting a glance over to her daughter.

To lads like Ryan, and to generations of local children, the ruins of the old Manor Lodge and the piece of rough wasteland that surrounds it has simply been known as 'Manor Castle'. Older, more intrepid children sometimes climb the time-worn stone wall and venture into the ruins of the old buildings themselves but there was always the danger of being caught by the grumpy custodian who lived in the ugly modern little house built specially on the site. The hills and hollows of the irregularly shaped fields on the hillside below the ruins, however, scarred with the debris of coal mining, still provide a playground of unparalleled opportunity for creative play. Here, in the long summer evenings, boys and girls are free to go wild and let imagination run riot, unrestricted by adult interference. It is a magical place, though few Sheffielders who live outside the Manor would suspect that here, in the heart of this downbeat estate, such a place exists. But the children know, and love it. They know that it is possible to push through the twining ivy, brambles and dog-roses to create a secret world, and that if they sit quietly, they may be lucky enough, like Ryan, to see one of the glittering grass snakes slither quickly into the open before disappearing once more. The girls, like Charlotte, know how to entice the friendly horses that live in the field below to come to the fence so that they can be fed and stroked.

But this is also a mysterious place, where it is possible to follow fresh wolf-prints in the wet mud and suspect that they are made by something half ape and half human or to wonder at the two strange, contorted shapes of the blocks of red clinker that stand on the hillside and cast weird shadows as the sun gets low in the sky. To the children, who use them as convenient posts for hide and seek, they are named 'The Lion' and 'The Crocodile'. And beneath the surface, hidden and forgotten, there are treasures to be found if you dig with a stick; pieces of broken pottery, bits of old clay pipes, rusty old metal objects and, if you are very lucky, maybe something really special like an old coin which once belonged to Mary Queen of Scots. Here it is easy to frighten less confident children with stories about ghosts heard wailing from behind the high walls or by telling them to watch out because 'Johnny's coming' or about the tunnels; everyone knows about the tunnels.

But of all the activities which Ryan and the other children enjoy on the waste ground, their very favourite is to build dens, and on this Saturday morning Ryan and his friends Joe and Bradley, who had called for him shortly after his mother had left, are busily engaged in dragging building materials up the hill to a spot behind the bushes against the ancient Manor wall. There is always plenty of useful material because there are those who use the deserted patch as an illegal tip. Today an old mattress and some worn carpet are being added to the secret shelter before the entrance is carefully concealed once more by pulling back the thick ivy growth between the trees, making it invisible to rival groups.

'My mum saw Spring-Heeled Jack last night,' said Ryan to Bradley as they dragged a piece of rusty corrugated iron into place.

'She saw what?' he replied.

'He's a ghost and he can jump right high and he's got a mask and a cape.'

'Sounds like she saw Batman,' mocked Joe.

It did sound a bit improbable, even to Ryan now, although it had seemed scary enough at the time. He decided not to mention it again.

It was another fortnight before Charlotte had the time to go and see her grandmother again. She was anxious to return the photograph that she had borrowed and to see what else there was in the fascinating box. It was strange that she had never seen it before but not surprising that her mother hadn't mentioned it, for she seemed to have little interest in the past. Charlotte, however, could not get the picture out of her mind. It had taken her completely by surprise and changed the way she saw her Gran. Until now she had never really thought of her Gran as anything but an old lady living alone in a cluttered flat. Now she realised that she had lived a whole life before Charlotte was even born. She found the idea a bit creepy. And there were pictures of other people in the box, people who she had never heard of but who were related to her and had lived and died before her. She longed to find out more about them. So on Saturday morning Charlotte walked down to Park Hill from her house on Manor Lane and called on Granny Velma.

'Oh hello duck,' said Gran, opening the door, 'do you want a biscuit?'

'No thanks Gran. I've brought that picture back. I wondered if you could show me the others in the box. I think they might help with my school work,' added Charlotte as she followed Velma into the living room.

'It's funny you should ask that. Since you got that old box of photographs out I've been having a look at them myself. Do you know I'd almost forgotten about some of them.'

The box was already open on the tablecloth and the pictures spread out. They sat down at the table and Velma began to pick them over.

'Did your mother tell you? There was a meeting last week about what the council are planning to do with the flats. These men came from London.'

'Do the plans look interesting then Gran?'

'Well, you know what they're like, these people. It was all talk. One was an American. What did he know about Sheffield? They showed us lots of fancy photos about what they plan to do to improve the outside but we said all we are really interested in is improving the inside of our flats. I'll believe it when I see it.'

Charlotte was listening with only half an ear. She was leafing through the old photos and came across a soldier. He stood smartly in a thick looking uniform, a white belt diagonally across his chest and stiff webbing wrapped around his legs. A waxed moustache that stuck out horizontally and made Charlotte giggle accentuated his stern expression.

'Who on earth is this Gran? It's not one of my relations is it?'

'It certainly is girl,' replied Gran, 'that's my great uncle Frank, and that's the last photograph that we've got of him. He had it taken just before he went to fight in the Great War. He was in the Sheffield Battalion, The "Sheffield Pals" they were called.'

'What happened to him?' asked Charlotte, fearing that she already knew the answer.

'He didn't come back, love, and neither did most of his mates. They were mown down on the Somme when they went over the top on July 1st 1916.'

Charlotte winced, feeling embarrassed that she had initially been amused by the uniformed figure that she now only saw as sad and heroic.

'And these are Frank's older sisters. The younger one, on the chair, is my grandmother,' said Velma, passing her another picture. 'She was called Alice.' This one was quite different. It was a stiff card, postcard sized, with a photographer's studio name, *Taylor, 21 Fargate, Sheffield*, in gold script at the bottom.

There were two little girls in the delightful photograph, one was about seven years old and was sitting looking very uncomfortable in a high-backed chair, whilst her older sister stood leaning against a small table. They were both dressed identically, from the ribbons which tied their long loose ringlets, to their spotless white pinafores and highly-polished high buttoned boots.

'Now *she* could have told you some stories right enough. She once told me about the time that a zeppelin came along Attercliffe in the First World War. She said it came along ever so slowly and dropped bombs as it went along. Some people were killed, I think. They didn't know to get out of the way in time!'

'Do you remember anything about the Second World War Gran?' asked Charlotte, suddenly remembering about Mrs Briggs and her project.

'Of course I do. Everybody that was here in Sheffield remembers the blitz. In fact the anti-aircraft battery was not far from where you live, down at the bottom of Manor Lane. They've built houses on it now. When those big guns started up they made such a din it brought the ceilings down in the houses on the Wybourn! I don't think they ever hit anything though.'

'Do you remember the bombing then?'

'Yes, duck. It was a Thursday night, 12th December 1940, not long before Christmas. I remember it well because I used to walk through town to get to work, just behind Atkinsons on the Moor. They had just put a beautiful display of all kinds of nuts in their window and, of course, the next day the whole place had gone. There was a land-mine destroyed a house near you, at the end of Manor Lane. Two men were killed there. One of them was the ARP Warden, Dickinson he was called. Come to think about it, there's a special memorial garden in the City Road Cemetery near your house. Many of the people who were killed in the blitz were buried there.'

'I'll get dad to take me to see it,' said Charlotte, 'I don't think Mrs Briggs knows about that.'

Just then the door opened, and in came Ryan with his mum. They had been Christmas shopping in town.

'Oh, I'm all in. It's packed in town, mother,' said Margaret, sighing and sitting down.

'I'll put the kettle on,' replied Velma, pottering out to the kitchen.

Ryan had his eye on the battered biscuit-tin sitting on the sideboard, and took the opportunity of his grandma's absence to take a peek inside. But it was not what he had been expecting. This tin contained not biscuits but buttons, dozens and dozens of them in every shape, colour, size and material imaginable.

'Oh yes, you've found my old button box I see,' said grandma coming back carrying a cup of tea. 'I found that in the bottom drawer yesterday.'

Charlotte and Ryan were fascinated by the eye-catching collection and were just about to tip them all out onto the table when their mother stopped them.

'We're not going to be long. Don't you two start making a mess.'

But something caught Charlotte's eye. It was round and light grey in colour, like a coin although it was not like any coin that she had ever seen before. On one side there was a picture of the Town Hall in the centre of Sheffield, and when she turned it over Charlotte read out the words *To Commemorate the 60th Year of the Reign of Queen Victoria On Her Visit to Open the Town Hall, May 21st, 1897. Duke of Norfolk, Mayor.* What's this Gran?'

'Why, I thought I'd lost that. It belonged to my grandma Alice. She was proud of that.'

'Well, thank you so much for bringing your great grandma's medal to show the class Charlotte,' said Mrs Briggs on Monday in school as the class sat on the carpet at the start of the literacy hour. 'You must take care not to lose this. I expect that it is quite precious, especially to your family.'

'Yes, my Gran has given it to me to keep now and I've found a special box to put it in. I keep it beside my bed with the photograph of my great great grandma Alice.'

Ryan, however, was having an uncomfortable morning. 'Miss Richards,' called Bradley, waving his hand in the air.

'Bradley will you please stop shouting at me like that. It is very rude. What is it anyway?'

'Miss, Ryan says his mum saw Spring-Heeled Jack the other night.' The children were sniggering and Ryan wished that he could have crawled away. 'What's that Miss? Do you believe in ghosts miss?'

'Stop teasing Ryan this minute, Bradley. You know that I won't have you making fun of other children. As it happens there's nothing funny about it. Lots of people in the past have said that they have seen a character with staring eyes who could leap over high walls. In Victorian times people got quite frightened to go out around Norfolk Park after dark because of it.'

'Did they ever catch him Miss.'

'No, and nobody knows if he was real or just a story,' replied Miss Richards, 'after all there are lots of stories about Park Hill you know, and it's often difficult to find out the real truth about them.' Miss Richards settled herself on her 'Literacy Chair.' 'Did I tell you the story of the tunnel that goes all the way from the old castle to the Manor Lodge?'

She had, of course, many times, but the children didn't let on. After all, the old stories are often the best.

POST-WAR REDEVELOPMENT

Although the area had been extensively cleared in 1937 it was not to be until the late 1950s that the re-planning of the area of lower Park Hill was boldly tackled. A revolutionary high-density development of 997 units was envisaged to create a multi-layered wall of dwellings linked by horizontal 'streets' at different levels. It was

Park Hill flats

hoped that in this way it would be possible to preserve the community cohesion which had existed previously. The concept came from the ideas of the French architect Le Corbusier and had not been attempted anywhere in this country previously. The first phase was completed in 1960 and Park Hill acquired the major new feature to its landscape which has characterised it ever since. It has always drawn controversy. Whilst becoming something of an architectural icon for groups of architectural students from all over the world it has never been popular with Sheffielders, and the recent decision to 'list' the decaying block as a building of major architectural merit has understandably fanned the embers. In some senses Park Hill has been a success and, despite maintenance problems and unforeseeable social problems that have created some hard times, Europe's first venture into deck access housing has remained popular with many of the original residents. Some have now lived here for over forty years and will be prepared to return when the refurbishment is complete.

The towers of the nearby Hyde Park development, which was higher and had access to the upper levels by lifts, made a very striking addition to the skyline but it was less successful, partly because the residents were not previously local and little community spirit devel-

Park Hill from the city centre in the 1970s

oped. Problems were such that, following a temporary refurbishment to house the athletes competing in the World Student Games in 1991, much of the complex was demolished. During the 1960s the process of covering the old Park with council housing was completed with the building of the Norfolk Park estate at its very heart and the extensive Gleadless Valley estates on its southern fringe, which until this late date had managed to retain its delightful rural nature amidst its surviving ancient woodlands. Here the skylarks still sang, the yellowhammers and linnets still flitted between gorse bushes and the kestrels hovered just as their ancestors had done in Anglo-Saxon times, by whom the area was named.

Acknowledgements

Many, many people have worked towards the creation of this book and we gratefully recognise their contributions:Project Manager, Clare Dykes, Green Estate Ltd; writer, Peter Machan; designers, Tony Williams & John Williams; photographer and researcher on the Manor Lodge, Steven Brownlow; researcher, Maureen Ogden.

Research: Nick Robinson and Mrs Shirt at the Sheffield office of the Duke of Norfolk; John Martin Robinson, archivist, and Sarah Roger, librarian, at Arundel Castle; Velma Robinson, Denise Ford, Edith Bradbury and Eileen Dale at Park Hill Tenants Association; Elizabeth Crowther, Ada Nixon, Mary Dyson and George Haywood for their life stories; Winifred Pepper, who still lives in John Holland's cottage; Erica Fidment and Kate Cossam for the research on Laithfield House; Christine Rose, Park Hill Housing Development Officer; Mrs Briggs and the children in her class (especially Charlotte and Ryan) at St. Oswald's Roman Catholic Community School; Jim Hurley of SIS Interior Solutions who has worked tirelessly for the restoration of the Cholera Monument; John Tait, warden at the Shrewsbury Hospital; Margaret Gardener, Anthony O'Connor and the Cathedral Guides; Kim Streets at Sheffield City Museum; Mike Spink and the staff at Sheffield Local Studies Library.

Thanks also to His Grace The Duke of Norfolk.

Picture Credits

The images are by Steven Brownlow, except for those listed below.:
Page 7, Ed Parsons; page 17, courtesy of J W Northend Ltd; pages 25 and 42, artist Martin Davenport, images courtesy of Sheffield Newspapers; page 38 and page 40 (top) by kind permission of His Grace The Duke of Norfolk; page 53, courtesy of Sheffield Galleries and Museums Trust; pages 57, 69 and 92, Peter Machan; page 58 (top), courtesy of Sheffield Galleries and Museums Trust; page 65, courtesy of Hadfield Cawkwell Davidson; page 89, Sheffield Galleries and Museums Trust; page 95, courtesy of Elizabeth Crowther.

The production of this book has been supported by Manor and Castle Development Trust, Single Regeneration Budget, Sheffield Wildlife Trust, Heritage Lottery Fund, The Area Panel for Manor, Castle and Woodthorpe and Manor Health Walks.

The Health Walks Project is part of a national scheme initiated by the Countryside Agency and the British Heart Foundation to help improve the health of people in local communities by encouraging walking in the local environment.

Bibliography

Joseph Hunter, *Hallamshire,* ed Gatty, (1869), the standard reference work, was used throughout,

as was Mary Walton's *Sheffield: Its Story and Its Achievements* (1948) and David Hey's *History of Sheffield* (1998).

Other major references include:

David Bostwick, *Sheffield in Tudor and Stuart Times* (1985)

D Durant, *Bess of Hardwick: Portrait of an Elizabethan Dynasty* (1977)

Sarah Gristwood, *Arbella: England's Lost Queen* (2003)

Mary Hervey, *The Life and Correspondence of Thomas Howard, Earl of Arundel* (1921).

Hugh Perry (publisher), *A Journal of Each Day's Passage of the Earl of Manchester's Army* (1664)

J M Robinson, *Arundel Castle*

R E Leader, *Sheffield in the Eighteenth Century* (1901)

T Walter Hall, *The Fairbanks of Sheffield* (1932)

Ian Medlicott, 'John Curr, Mining Engineer and Viewer' in *Aspects of Sheffield 2* (1999)

Stokes, *The Cholera Epidemic in Sheffield* (1920)

Thomas Shapter, *The History of the Cholera in Exeter* (1832)

Haywood and Lee, *The Sheffield Sanitary Report* (1867)

Friends of Norfolk Heritage Park, various recent publications

'Queen Victoria's Visit to Sheffield' in *Sheffield and Rotherham Independent* (May 21st and 22nd 1897)

Park Local History Group, *Park Reflections* (1995)

Architectural Association (publisher), *Park Hill, What Next?* (1996)

Many internet sites will give you further information about Spring-Heeled Jack.

Look especially at *Spring Time for Sheffield* by Martin Jeffery at www.mysterymag.com

To reach the start of the trail, turn off City Road, up Manor Lane (by Manor Lodge School). Continue to the top of hill where you will see the great chimney of Manor Lodge. Manor Lodge is well served by public transport (buses 41 and 95) and also lies close to the Trans-Pennine Trail.

1 The Trail begins at Sheffield Manor Lodge, the most significant remaining piece of Sheffield's history; where Mary Queen of Scots, the Norfolks and the Shrewsburys, hundreds of years of industry and the lives of the present day community, come together.

2 From Manor Lodge turn right along Manor Lane and then left onto Harwich Road which leads to the northern entrance of the City Road Cemetery (built in 1881). Cross the cemetery, heading towards your right and leave by the main City Road entrance.

3 Alternative Route: cross directly over the road from Manor Lodge and walk down Manor Park Crescent, into Manor Fields Park and round the back of the Cemetery. Either route will bring you out on City Road

4 From the Cemetery main entrance, cross over City Road at the pedestrian lights below, turn down the footpath between houses and follow the path down the hill.

5 Enter Norfolk Heritage Park through entrances at St Aidan's Avenue or Guildford Avenue. At Centre in the Park you will find a café and other facilities. From the park entrance turn right and follow the tree-lined avenue straight down to the Granville Road exit.

6 Cross over the pedestrian crossing and follow Granville Road downhill for approx 200 yards. Follow the signs or turn right up Norfolk Road. Either following a marked path through Clay Woods or up Norfolk Road you will reach Cholera Monument Grounds where there are beautiful views of the city from the recently restored 71ft Monument.

7 Leave Cholera Monument Grounds by the Norfolk Road exit: the old Shrewsbury Hospital is opposite you as you leave. Turn left down Norfolk Road and left again down Shrewsbury Road. Turn right into South Street Park at the Sweet Factory and follow the paths down to the tram-line. Cross over the tram-lines and follow the footpath right, below Park Hill flats. The route continues alongside the tram-line, over Park Square roundabout and uphill along Commercial Street, still following the tram-lines.

8 Diversions: As the Trail passes through Fitzalan Square there are historical features to left and right. You can turn right down Waingate to the site of Sheffield Castle – though in truth there is little to see, as most of the remnants are hidden from public view under modern developments; or turn left along Flat Street to find the Old Queen's Head, the pub housed in Sheffield's oldest surviving domestic dwelling.

9 The trail continues uphill and ends at Sheffield Cathedral on Church Street in the city centre. The Cathedral is home to the Shrewsbury Chapel.